Lex Naturalis

A Journal of Natural Law   Volume 2   Fall 2016

Copyright © 2016
Pace University Press
41 Park Row, 15th Floor
New York, NY 10038

ISBN: 978-1-935625-99-5
ISSN: 2474-8994

Walter Raubicheck
Editor

Editorial Board

Harold Brown
Department of Philosophy & Religious Studies, Pace University

Michael Baur
Department of Philosophy, Fordham University

James M. Jacobs
Notre Dame Seminary, New Orleans

Gregory J. Kerr
Department of Philosophy & Theology, DeSales University

Robert Chapman
Department of Philosophy and Environmental Studies, Pace University

Alice Ramos
Department of Philosophy, St. John's University

Peter Widulski
School of Law, Pace University

Lex Naturalis

CONTENTS

VOLUME 2   **FALL 2016**

FEATURED ARTICLES

Locating *Laudato Si'* Along a Catholic Trajectory of Concern for Animals	Charles Camosy	1
Anthropocentrism and Integral Ecology in Germain Grisez's Natural Law	Jacaranda Turvey Tait	21
Does Natural Law Dictate Care for the Environment Solely on Human-Centered Grounds?	Marie George	43
The Rational Order of Nature and the Environmental Implications of Natural Law	James M. Jacobs	65
Laudato Si': A Natural Law Ethic of Care	Michael Dauphinais	87
Natural Law and the Imitation of Nature: A Thomistic Development of Human Ecology	Scott Jude Roniger	111

BOOK REVIEWS

Review of *Conscience and its Enemies: Confronting the Dogmas of Liberal Secularism* by Robert George (Intercollegiate Studies Institute, 2016) Matthew Minerd 131

Review of *Knowing the Natural Law: From Precepts and Inclinations to Deriving Oughts* by Steven J. Jensen (The Catholic University of America Press 2015) James M. Jacobs 135

Review of *Two Years Eight Months and Twenty-Eight Nights* by Salman Rushdie (Random House 2015) Richard Douglas Connerney 139

CONTRIBUTORS 143

CALL FOR PAPERS 145

LOCATING *LAUDATO SI'* ALONG A CATHOLIC TRAJECTORY OF CONCERN FOR NON-HUMAN ANIMALS

Charles Camosy

INTRODUCTION

Once dismissed as a fringe topic for activists and extremists, concern for the moral and legal status of non-human animals is exploding throughout Western culture. Major documentaries like CNN's "Blackfish" run in primetime and lead directly to the kind of pressure which forces previously untouchable organizations like Sea World to radically change their relationship to orcas.[1] Major news coverage of how elephants and other animals are decimated by the ivory trade led to the United States proposing a ban.[2] Denmark is now even proposing a special tax on beef and other meats in order to combat this kind of consumption's disproportionate contribution to climate change.[3] The move to plant-based diets, particularly as a response to the horrific suffering of billions and billions of animals in factory farming, has gone mainstream.[4]

One could make a strong argument that this is the result of the decades of attention these issues have received from moral philosophy. Peter Singer, in particular, as perhaps the most influential philosopher over the last forty years, has driven the arguments, interest, and concern for the topic. His *Animal Liberation* kicked off the beginning of an era in which philosophers and activists worked together to bring attention to an issue that was previously neglected.[5] The growing level of support and urgency they created then led to important books like J.M. Coetzee's *The Lives of Animals* and Jonathan Safran Foer's *Eating Animals*, which would bring the concern to whole new audiences.[6]

It look much longer for the issue to get off the ground in moral theology. As John Berkman and Celia Deane-Drummond note in their introduction to a recent edition of the *Journal of Moral Theology* which is completely devoted to non-human animals (the first of its kind), only a decade ago the little Catholic work that was being done on animal ethics was widely dismissed and even ridiculed.[7] Berkman recounted a disturbing story where, as a pre-tenure professor at the Catholic University of America, he had actually been ordered by his department chair to stop writing on the topic. Deane-Drummond reported being mocked by major figures in moral theology when she gave a paper on the topic at a major conference. I know from my own experience writing on the topic how difficult it has been to bring up animals as an issue of concern in the context of Catholic theology.

But in just the past few years, the moral-theological landscape has shifted dramatically. Not only has there been an entire issue of a respected journal devoted to the topic (featuring eminent theologians like Jean Porter and Julie Hanlon-Rubio), but the Society of Christian Ethics (SCE)—in addition to regularly featuring concurrent sessions on the topic—recently approved a special "Animal Ethics" interest group for the annual convention. Stanley Hauerwas' presidential address at the 2012 SCE convention was dominated by his reflections on Coetzee's concern for animals. David Clough, a moral theologian who has devoted most of his career to concern for animals, was named president of the United Kingdom's Society for the Study of Christian Ethics and devoted the 2016 annual conference to this topic. Perhaps the most important living Catholic theologian, Elizabeth Johnson, recently completed an entire book on the topic of non-human animals.[8] Simply put, attention to this topic has gone from marginalized to prime time in virtually the blink of an eye.

This is no mere "niche" concern on the theological and political left. Indeed, the pro-life movement is now starting to embrace concern for animals as a significant issue. John Berkman and I have both written on the topic from a pro-life perspective,[9] and we've been joined by people like the Ethics and Public Policy Center's Mary Eberstadt and former speech-writer for George W. Bush, Matthew Scully.[10] Most importantly, Pope Francis has connected concern for animals, and ecological concern more generally, with his pro-life commitments.[11]

In this article I will argue that in promulgating *Laudato Si'*, Pope Francis has laid down a significant marker along the trajectory of Catholic concern for non-human animals. This marker signals an important shift away from the approach of the post-Vatican II era, and a return to scriptural and traditional resources which are much friendlier to animals. I will set up this trajectory beginning with scriptural and historical highlights and then turn to contemporary discussions with a focus on Vatican II, St. John Paul II, and Pope Benedict XVI, and the *Catechism of the Catholic Church*. This will lead us to the *Laudato Si'* moment, which I will examine in some detail. Finally, I will suggest some ways the conversation might go from here.

At each level of the argument, I will have three central organizing ideas that will be of special concern:

1. How should we think about the **moral status** of non-human animals? Do animals have inherent value or can we ultimately link moral concern about animals to human concerns and interests? How, if at all, are animals morally distinct from the rest of creation? How, if at all, are they distinct from each other?

2. When thinking about concern for animals, how should we think about **anthropocentrism?** Post-Vatican II theology problematically lifts up the human animal to the exclusion of the non-human animal, but can the proper response be to eliminate anthropocentrism altogether? Is it possible to speak about a "soft" anthropocentrism which at once preserves the hierarchical tradition while giving due weight to non-human animals?

3. Given the clear moral-theological commitments of the tradition on this topic, should there be any **practical guidance** for how we are to treat non-human animals in specific circumstances?

THE TRAJECTORY OF CONCERN
LEADING UP TO *LAUDATO SI'*[12]

From the very first page of scripture, we learn that animals were created "good," period. Their value comes from God creating them as the kinds of things that they are, not from their usefulness to human beings. Even in Genesis 2, when God brings the animals to human beings, it is because "it is not good man should be alone." Human animals, though created on the same day as non-human animals (and, according to Ecclesiastes 3:19, sharing the same breath of life), are special because God has made them in God's own image and after God's likeness. We have been given dominion and rule over the earth and the other animals have not.

But Christians are to interpret this kind of dominion and rule through the Lordship of Jesus Christ, a dominion characterized by servanthood, self-emptying, and sacrifice. Whatever this dominion over creation might mean, it is anything but a license to dominate and exploit. This dominion must be consistent not only with God's bringing the animals to Adam because he was alone, but also with God, at the end of Genesis 1, giving all animals (human and non-human) a vegetarian diet. According to the creation story, God's original creation is a place of deathless non-violence.

Of course, the same creation story reveals that this beautiful creation was sullied by the sin of human beings, and with sin came violence and death. It is only after sin that God first gives human beings limited permission to kill and eat animals. Nevertheless, Christians are to witness the return of the Peaceable Kingdom, which the prophet Isaiah claims will see lambs lie down with lions and babies play with snakes. Why, then, do so many claim that animals were created by God for our use and exploitation? And why is scripture invoked to defend it? David Clough calls this the "it's all about us" position, and blames it on both self-interest and an uncritical acceptance of the influence of Platonic, Gnostic, and Stoic thought.[13] But if one's view is grounded in scripture, then one comes to a much more complex conclusion about the right relationship between human and non-human animals.

This tension between Scripture and the "it's all about us" position, however, came to dominate much of the tradition. Many of the early Church fathers were outspokenly in favor of "it's all about us," but at the same time were strongly critical of Christian participation in sport hunting and going to the Roman games where animals were slaughtered for the entertainment of the crowd.[14] The historian Thomas Wiedermann notes that early Christian leaders were concerned about the effect that witnessing the violence would have on spectators. In the view of Tertullian, for instance, repeated watching of exotic wild animals from around the Empire fighting each other to death turned the crowd into "savages." Gregory of Nazianzen considered "men killing one another" and "the slaughter of wild beasts" on the same list of problems with the games themselves. Basil the Great criticized the "wealthy men" who for "secular honor" make men fight wild beasts.[15]

But about what, precisely, were these great Church leaders worried? Consider that it was not unheard of to have over 10,000 non-human animals killed during a single celebration season: from tigers, to elephants, to pythons, to bears, to crocodiles. Would they have been similarly concerned about their fellow Christians watching, say, 10,000 trees get hacked to death? Of course not. It was precisely the high moral status of the non-human animals being killed which caused those who witnessed thousands of their vicious and violent deaths to become savages.

And the tension would persist. Despite being mentored by Albert the Great, the most prominent zoologist of the Middle Ages, Thomas Aquinas would have little to say about animals. What he did say, however, was full of tension. On the one hand, following Aristotle, he insisted non-human animals did not have a rational soul and on this basis argued that they cannot, strictly speaking, be wronged. It can be wrong for human persons (who do have rational souls) to treat animals with cruelty, but ultimately the wrong we do is to ourselves by acting counter to virtue. Several centuries later, Peter Singer would lift up Thomas Aquinas' disproportionate influence as a primary reason he considered the Christian tradition an enemy of animal protection. This is a position he has since abandoned, however.[16]

On the other hand, Thomas also insisted that the highest good after God is not the good of human beings, but rather the good of all creation. Indeed, he ranks humans lowest on the hierarchy of rational beings. Furthermore, as John Berkman has pointed out, Thomas believed that non-human animals share with human animals a spiritual reality or soul.[17] There are a host of activities which human and non-human animals perform "without rationality" as Thomas understood the term. In addition to learning certain motor skills, memorizing information for a test, or even making a sandwich, Berkman and certain other Thomistic thinkers believe that even for Thomas animals "have a reason" for doing what they do. An animal soul can also know and feel via emotions like fear, hate, joy, anger, sympathy, and indignation. Jean Porter points out that that these emotions, as Thomas understood them, were strongly related to moral capacity.[18]

The tension between "it's all about us" and a more Scriptural position on animals would persist from the Middle Ages through the manualist tradition of moral theology in the late nineteenth and early twentieth centuries. Indeed, Berkman argues the manuals took animals seriously in a way that the humanism of Vatican II and its successor movements in moral theology would simply ignore. Shockingly, if you do a word search for "animal" in *Gaudium et Spes*—Vatican II's major work on the Church in the modern world—you will find exactly zero entries. To make matters worse, Chapter One begins with this unfortunate sentence: "According to the almost unanimous opinion of believers and unbelievers alike, all things on earth should be related to man as their center and crown." It may have been correct to say this was the opinion of nearly all people in 1965, but it is not an opinion grounded in scripture and the tradition of the Church. After Vatican II, we have a collapse of the tension in favor of the "it's all about us" position. As Berkman laments, moral theologians after the Council—even among those interested in ecology and care for creation more broadly—"ignored both the general issue of human responsibilities to non-human animals, and the specific issue of animal cruelty."[19]

The pontificates of St. John Paul II and Benedict XVI, however, would go a long way to reclaiming the tension. Everyone who knows Benedict well, for instance, is aware that he is a huge animal lover and as Pope had to be reminded that he could not take in stray cats from the surrounding Roman streets. PETA took advantage of this fact and promoted his words in their advertisements. One flier that got a lot of public attention focused on his response to a question asked of him by German journalist Peter Seewald not long before he became Pope, when he was in charge of safeguarding Catholic doctrine. Seewald asked, "Are we allowed to make use of animals, and even to eat them?" His response would eventually become the basis of a PETA advertisement:

> That is a very serious question. At any rate, we can see that they are given into our care, that we cannot just do whatever we want with them. Animals, too, are God's creatures. Certainly, a sort of industrial use of creatures, so that geese are fed in such a way as to produce as large a liver as possible, or hens live so packed together that they become just caricatures of birds, this degrading of living creatures to a commodity seems to me in fact to contradict the relationship of mutuality that comes across in the Bible.[20]

St. John Paul II, invoking St. Francis on the 800th anniversary of his death, said, "It is necessary and urgent that with the example of the little poor man from Assisi, one decides to abandon unadvisable forms of domination, the locking up of all creatures."[21] He would go on to publish a new *Catechism of the Catholic Church*, which had very interesting things to say about animals. It leads off in paragraph #703 by citing the aforementioned chapter of Ecclesiastes in claiming both humans and animals have the breath of life. But the most detailed teaching is in paragraphs 2416-2418:

> Animals are God's creatures. He surrounds them with his providential care. By their mere existence they bless him and

give him glory. Thus men owe them kindness. We should recall the gentleness with which saints like St. Francis of Assisi or St. Philip Neri treated animals. God entrusted animals to the stewardship of those whom he created in his own image. Hence it is legitimate to use animals for food and clothing. They may be domesticated to help man in his work and leisure. It is contrary to human dignity to cause animals to suffer or die needlessly.

This passage leaves no doubt but that the tension has returned to a Catholic understanding of animals. The Biblical view that God cares about non-human animals is stressed; but then, quite interestingly, we see that it is precisely because of God's providential care that we human beings owe non-human animals kindness. Very strong language is used. Indeed, it is the language of *justice* that is used: we *owe* animals kindness.

Then comes the tension: the *Catechism* rightly points out that God has entrusted human beings with the care and stewardship of non-human animals, but this apparently goes beyond caring for the well-being and flourishing of such animals. We are told that they may be used for food and clothing and may be domesticated for help with work or leisure. This has much more in common with "it's all about us." But the very next line prohibits causing non-human animals to "suffer or die needlessly." The use of animals is limited not only by our obligation to show them kindness, but we are also told not to cause them to suffer or die unless doing so rises to the level of need. Unfortunately, the *Catechism* gives us no suggestions for what might be an example of the kind of need which could justify causing an animal to suffer or die.

So what can we say about the three central issues that are the focus of this article?

1. **Moral Status.** We know that animals are not mere things which exist to be used by humans. God created them good, cares about their welfare, and asks us to care for their welfare as well. But they don't rise to the level of persons, who are ends in themselves and can never be radically reduced as a mere means to an end. In

short, the trajectory of Catholic thinking on this question leading up to *Laudato Si'* is ambiguous.

2. **Anthropocentrism.** While it is clear humans have a special place in God's created order, being created in the image of God, we do not hold the highest place. And while human beings hold a higher place in creation than do non-human animals, non-human animals still hold a higher place than does the rest of creation, and make significant moral claims on human beings.

3. **Practical guidance.** While some general norms are put in place, we are not given practical guidance about how to treat animals in specific situations. It may seem obvious that eating meat for pleasure doesn't rise to the level of "need," while doing medical experiments on mice to cure cancer does meet the standard, but this kind of guidance simply isn't forthcoming.

This leads up to the present where, as mentioned above, there is good but relatively new work being done by theologians on these questions. Many of us were looking to the summer 2015 release of *Laudato Si'* to push the tradition forward on what is becoming an urgent set of questions for our culture.

POPE FRANCIS AND *LAUDATO SI'*

Perhaps the central theme of Pope Francis' encyclical on *Our Common Home* is that of "integral ecology." Invoking Francis of Assisi, the Pope argues we must adopt his deep connection to the whole of creation:

> If we approach nature and the environment without this openness to awe and wonder, if we no longer speak the language of fraternity and beauty in our relationship with the world, our attitude will be that of masters, consumers, ruthless exploiters, unable to set limits on their immediate needs. By contrast, if we feel intimately united with all that exists, then sobriety and care will well up spontaneously. The poverty and austerity of Saint Francis were no mere veneer of asceticism, but something much more radical: a refusal to turn reality into an object simply to be used and controlled.[22]

If it is truly an integral approach, Pope Francis says we must be radically aware of how interconnected human beings are to the rest of creation. Thinking of "the environment" as something radically separate from ourselves risks "fragmentation of knowledge" that leads to "a kind of ignorance."[23]

But especially given the close connection between human and non-human animals—both socially and genetically (Francis specifically brings up the latter metric as quite significant[24])—it is striking how little explicit attention the encyclical gives to non-human animals. This is particularly surprising, not only given how much attention the topic has received in the years leading up the encyclical, but also because this Pope named himself after the greatest animal lover of all time, Francis of Assisi. In what follows, I will lay out the few but significant places where *Laudato Si'* takes on either something specific about non-human animals, or something so directly related that it bears mentioning. I will then comment on some significant omissions—omissions that are even more significant given the framework and goals of the encyclical. I will conclude the article by making an argument on "where we need to go from here" in the trajectory of Catholic thought on non-human animals.

The encyclical does offer significant thoughts on the moral status of non-human animals, even if it not as clear as it might have been. There is, for instance, quite strong language used when it comes to preservation of biodiversity. Such diversity, the Pope said, is good for human beings, but it is a mistake to "think of different species merely as potential 'resources' to be exploited, while overlooking the fact that they have value in themselves."[25] While reinforcing the Biblical view that creation has value in itself, parts of *Laudato Si'* are explicitly skeptical of making distinctions between creatures. While it may "disturb us to learn of the extinction of mammals or birds," Pope Francis urges us to nevertheless focus our attention on "the good functioning" of "fungi, algae, worms, insects, reptiles and an innumerable variety of microorganisms" as well.[26] There are several other passages which drive home this point:

> "We must forcefully reject the notion that our being created in God's image and given dominion over the earth justifies absolute domination over other creatures."[27]
>
> Creation has "an intrinsic value" which is "independent of [its] usefulness. Each organism, as a creature of God, is good and admirable in itself."[28]

But these passages make no distinctions between creatures. To what do phrases like "other creatures" and "each organism" refer? Does the Pope mean to say that fungi and insects are on the same moral level as dolphins and chimpanzees?

While in the above passages it seems the answer is yes, in other places the answer is more ambiguous. For instance, in a striking section in which he invokes Mary, Francis says the following:

> Mary, the Mother who cared for Jesus, now cares with maternal affection and pain for this wounded world. Just as her pierced heart mourned the death of Jesus, so now she grieves for the sufferings of the crucified poor and for the creatures of this world laid waste by human power.[29]

Again, precisely what is being said here isn't clear, but the passage seems to focus on pain and suffering in a way that suggests those creatures who are capable of pain and suffering are of particular concern for the Blessed Mother. However, a reasonable person could also read this passage as her being pained for literally all creatures who are laid waste by human power, from algae to elephants. The text supports either reading.

Much media attention was paid to *Laudato Si'* coming down on the side of animals making it to the afterlife.[30] But here also the ambiguity remains stubborn. Francis claims that "each creature," "resplendently transfigured," will have a shared experience of eternal life.[31] On the one hand, it just isn't clear what it would mean for microorganisms to have experiences of anything, so this passage seems to privilege creatures who can have experiences. But when read through the lens suggested by the previous passages, again, a reasonable person could take a wide view of what is meant by "each creature." Frustratingly, as we will see in more detail below, the encyclical is only clear about the special status of animals when it quotes the *Catechism*.[32]

One clear hierarchy present in the encyclical, however, is the distinction between human beings and the rest of creation. On the one hand, a "hard" anthropocentrism is very clearly ruled out by Francis given his underlining creation's inherent dignity, independent of its value for human beings. What the Pope describes as a "distorted" understanding of the dominion God has given us over creation, one which refuses to acknowledge this inherent value, is under fierce assault throughout the encyclical. On the other hand, it is just as clear that humans have a special place in creation, having been created in the image and likeness of God, and priority is given to human concerns. For instance, of the several sections present in Francis' discussion of "integral ecology," only one section is concerned explicitly with non-human concerns. What one might call a "soft" anthropocentrism is present in the other sections, in which Francis focuses on issues like the economics, intergenerational justice, and "daily life" of human beings. It is also worth noting how Francis decides to quote the *Catechism* on animals. He doesn't even mention the teaching that human beings "owe animals kindness," and instead focuses on the anthropocentric idea that our mistreatment of animals is mistaken because it is "contrary to human dignity."[33]

There are other places, however, where Francis appears to downplay even a soft anthropocentrism. He claims, for instance, that the "disappearance of a culture can be just as serious, or even more serious, than the disappearance of a species of plant or animal."[34] It is once again less than clear what is being said here, but this could reasonably be read as the Pope being unsure about whether the disappearance of a human culture could be on par with the disappearance of, say, a species of fern or rat. It could also be read as the Pope suggesting that the existence of culturally-specific practices (like, say, whale-hunting or seal clubbing) could trump the existence of a non-human species. But the very fact there is ambiguity here sends an interesting message in itself.

Perhaps unsurprisingly, given how little Francis said about non-human animals in the abstract, there is also little practical guidance to be found in *Laudato Si'* for how we are to treat them in specific circumstances. One exception involves a brief discussion of the use of animals in biomedical research, and it is worth quoting:

> While human intervention on plants and animals is permissible when it pertains to the necessities of human life, the *Catechism of the Catholic Church* teaches that experimentation on animals is morally acceptable only 'if it remains within reasonable limits [and] contributes to caring for or saving human lives.' The *Catechism* firmly states that human power has limits and that 'it is contrary to human dignity to cause animals to suffer or die needlessly.' All such use and experimentation 'requires a religious respect for the integrity of creation.'

Again, the use of the *Catechism* here is selective; no mention is made of the fact that it also teaches that we owe animals kindness. For those seeking moral guidance with respect to how they should treat animals in a biomedical context, the language is hopelessly vague. Lots of people who agree that research on animals ought to be done only for "the necessities of human life" within "reasonable limits" will nevertheless radically disagree about what sort of research protocols that would require.

Shockingly, at least for those of us who work on animal ethics, there is nothing explicit in the encyclical about factory farming. There is a reference to the need to support smaller farms,[35] and such a move would, of necessity, move us away from the business model of monstrously large factory farms which conceived of animals as nothing more than an opportunity to grow the maximum amount of protein units per square foot. But nothing at all is said about the billions and billions of animals haplessly tortured and killed in these farms. This social structure of sin intersects with so many concerns of the encyclical. From the biotechnology used to breed the feeling of satiation out of chickens, to the horrific treatment of workers, to the creation of super-drug-resistant bacteria, to the huge contribution these farms make to climate change, it would be difficult to come up with a topic more in need of a critique coming from the encyclical's commitment to integral ecology. And yet, inexplicably, we find no direct mention of the practice.

We are also given no tools to make distinctions in our treatment of specific creatures. When Francis says, "Each organism, as a creature of God, is good and admirable in itself; the same is true of the harmonious ensemble of organisms existing in a defined space and functioning as a system," again, it looks as if he is shying away from a moral hierarchy of creatures. But aren't there moral distinctions to be made between biomedical research which kills fungi and research which (painfully) kills cats? Aren't there moral distinctions to be made between our decisions to eat a genetically modified orange and a genetically modified chicken? Remarkably, *Laudato Si'* gives us no direct reason to answer these questions in the affirmative.

WHERE WE MIGHT GO FROM HERE

Laudato Si' did make one important thing quite clear. It firmly rejects the peculiar (post) Vatican II's emphasis on the special moral status of human beings—an emphasis which excluded moral consideration of non-human animals. When a Pope writes an encyclical so firmly on the side of the pre-Vatican II tension discussed above, it is difficult to see how the Church could ever go back to the bad old days of utter exclusion of non-human animals from serious consideration. Beyond this, however, *Laudato Si'* does not make many clear advances in the conversation. In concluding this article, I suggest some directions in which Catholic thinking could go that would address some pressing questions and gaps.

At a foundational level, apart from any consideration of humans, the tradition must come to grips with the moral status of non-human animals compared with the rest of creation. Nearly everyone has the strong intuition that killing and eating a head of lettuce because it gives us pleasure is a fundamentally different moral act from killing and eating a dog because it gives us pleasure. Is such an intuition morally justified? Yes? Then what, precisely, justifies a hierarchy of moral status among the many entities in creation? Does this have implications for how we are to think about the moral status of different kinds of animals? Again, most of us have a strong intuition that using a chimpanzee in a medical experiment is a very different thing from using a mouse. What, if anything, justifies our thinking this way?

We also need to think hard about the kind of moral obligation that such a moral status demands of us. The *Catechism* uses the language of justice on the one hand (animals are "owed" something from us) and the language of virtue (treating animals poorly violates *human* dignity) on the other. Is it one or the other? Is it both? Some Christian ethicists claim that justice only applies to human beings and could never apply to animals, while others claim that the specific wrong done to animals when they are treated with cruelty violates a clear duty of justice we have to them.[36] Especially if some non-human animals have a high moral status, more reflection is needed on the precise kind of wrong that is involved in treating them with cruelty.

Another tension (or at least uncertainty) in the *Catechism* comes with its claim that we must not cause animals to "suffer or die needlessly." Pope Francis also says in *Laudato Si'* that the Genesis narrative "implies a relationship of mutual responsibility between human beings and nature" and that we human beings may take what only what our community "needs for subsistence."[37] But what is meant by the use of the term "need," in either context, is simply not clear. On the one hand, the *Catechism* seems to imply that this is consistent with eating animals, using them for clothing, and for research, labor, and entertainment. But on the other hand we are told to treat animals with kindness. Is there ever a context in which it is *kind* to an animal to kill him and wear his skin? Or does the term "kind" only refer to the manner in which we kill (and perhaps grow and house) the animal?

The tension between "being kind to animals" on the one hand, and "taking from them what we need" on the other, is a specific example of the general kind of tension between the Scriptural position and the "it's all about us" position. Part of how this gets resolved in any particular case will involve the moral status of the animal or animals involved. It also depends in part on answers to the questions of anthropocentrism engaged above. If one has the "its all about us" position, then "needlessly" might be interpreted here as "thoughtlessly" or "recklessly." But if one has a softer anthropocentrism, one more in tune with *Laudato Si'*, then "needlessly" sounds like a much higher threshold to meet. Since our duty is to care for animals as God's creatures, not ours, then that which could justify using animals for our own purposes would be an actual need, like health care or disease prevention. Killing them simply because they taste good, or because they look good on us when we wear them, wouldn't meet the requirement. A certain kind of anthropocentrism, based on the fact that God creates human beings in God's image and likeness, is an essential part of the tradition. But spelling out how "hard" or "soft" that anthropocentrism is—particularly when it comes to our relationship with other animals—is an important direction for further work.

Especially after *Laudato Si'*, we are also left wondering about the implications of the fact that Christians are to witness a peaceable creation of harmony and nonviolence. The Kingdom of God is not yet fully realized, obviously, yet the Pope says this:

> It is significant that the harmony which Saint Francis of Assisi experienced with all creatures was seen as a healing of that rupture. Saint Bonaventure held that, through universal reconciliation with every creature, Saint Francis in some way returned to the state of original innocence. This is a far cry from our situation today, where sin is manifest in all its destructive power in wars, the various forms of violence and abuse, the abandonment of the most vulnerable, and attacks on nature.[38]

Is Pope Francis asking us here to live as witnesses to the original state of non-violence in Eden? If so, this means living in a non-violent relationship with non-human animals. God gave us dominion over them, yes, but also gave us a vegetarian diet. More work needs to be done in thinking about whether Christians are called to live toward a Genesis 2 world in which God brings the animals to us because it is not good for us to be alone, or a Genesis 9 world in which we inspire "fear and dread" in other animals.

Finally, it is long past time that some direct moral claims be made about specific practices with regard to non-human animals. Regardless of how we answer the above difficult questions, there are some practices so terrible that they ought to be directly and forcefully condemned, even at this early stage of the conversation. Genesis 2 is strong evidence that companion animals are legitimate, but surely a very basic commitment to the welfare of animals prohibits spending huge sums of money on "show" pets who have been bred in horrific conditions.[39] Even if one comes to a conclusion that eating some meat is morally acceptable, surely the kind of profit-centered breeding of factory-farmed chickens so that they feel constantly hungry is a cruelty which goes beyond the pale. Expert marksmen hunting animals so that they don't starve during the winter is a morally defensible practice, but hungover weekend warriors shooting deer in the stomach and causing a long, painful death is a terrible way to accomplish this goal. Using animals in medical research is perhaps the best example of use that rises to the level of "need," but current biomedical research practices are now pushing toward fundamental manipulation of animals, creating them as mere tools of research that in no way respects them as belonging to God rather than to us.[40]

The tradition has been quite clear in giving specific moral guidance with respect to actions which clearly contradict the fundamental dignity of human beings. It is high time similar guidance is given with respect to actions which clearly contradict the fundamental dignity of non-human animals.

NOTES

1. Amena Schelling, "Sea World Explains Why it Stops Breeding Orcas," https://www.thedodo.com/seaworld-breeding-ban-reason-1702760044.html 17 May 2016.
2. Kate Gibson, "Proposed US Ban on Ivory Faces Powerful Foe," http://www.cbsnews.com/news/proposed-u-s-ban-on-ivory-trade-faces-powerful-foe/ 17 May 2016.
3. "Denmark Considers Tax on Beef and Other Red Meat to Combat Climate Change," http://www.foxnews.com/leisure/2016/04/27/denmark-considers-tax-on-beef-other-red-meats-to-combat-climate-change/ 17 May 2016.
4. Elizabeth Crawford, "Vegan is Going Mainstream, Trend Data Suggests," http://www.foodnavigator-usa.com/Markets/Vegan-is-going-mainstream-trend-data-suggests.
5. Peter Singer, *Animal Liberation* (Harper Collins, 1975).
6. J.M. Coetzee, *The Lives of Animals* (Princeton University Press, 1999) and Jonathan Safran Foer, *Eating Animals* (Little, Brown, and Company, 2009).
7. John Berkman and Celia Deane-Drummond, "Catholic Moral Theology and the Moral Status of Non-Human Animals," *Journal of Moral Theology* (3) 2 June 2014.
8. Elizabeth Johnson, *Ask the Beasts: Darwin and the God of Love* (Bloomsbury, 2014).
9. John Berkman, "Prophetically Pro-Life: Pope John Paul II's Gospel of Life and Evangelical Concern for Animals," *Josephinum Journal of Theology* (1) 6 1999. Charles Camosy, *For Love of Animals: Christian Ethics, Consistent Action* (Franciscan, 2013).
10. Mary Eberstadt, "Pro-Animal, Pro-Life," http://www.firstthings.com/article/2009/06/pro-animal-pro-life and Matthew Scully, "Pro-Life, Pro-Animal," http://www.nationalreview.com/article/359761/pro-life-pro-animal-matthew-scully.
11. "Since everything is interrelated, concern for the protection of nature is also incompatible with the justification of abortion. How can we genuinely teach the importance of concern for other vulnerable beings, however troublesome or inconvenient they may be, if we fail to protect a human embryo, even when its presence is uncomfortable and creates difficulties? 'If personal and social sensitivity towards the acceptance of the new life is lost, then other forms of acceptance that are valuable for society also wither away.'" *Laudato Si'*, #120.
12. Some of this material comes from my book *For Love of Animals: Christian Ethics: Consistent Action* (Franciscan, 2013).
13. David Clough, *On Animals: Systematic Theology* (T&T Clark, 2012).
14. See, for instance, Jerome's commentary on Ps 90.3: "Esau was a hunter because he was a sinner. In the Holy Scriptures we do not find any saints who

are hunters." (quoted in Short, William, 'Animal Symbolism', in *Encyclopedia of the Bible and Its Reception*, Allison Jr. D., C. Helmer, S. McKenzie, T. Römer, J. Schröter, Seow C., Walfish B., and Ziolkowski E. (eds.), (Berlin: de Gruyter, 2009). Also, see St. Cyril of Jerusalem, who says "Now the pomp of the devil is the madness of theatres, and horse-races, and hunting, and all such vanity: from which that holy man praying to be delivered says unto God, 'Turn away mine eyes from beholding vanity.'" ("Five Catechetical Lectures to the Newly Baptized," Lecture 19, §6, in *A Select Library of Nicene and Post-Nicene Fathers of the Christian Church*, Second Series, Philip Schaff (ed.), (Edinburgh: T & T Clark, 1997), vol. 7.

15. Thomas Wiederman, *Emperors and Gladiators* (Routledge, 1995).
16. http://www.nytimes.com/2013/12/07/us/exploring-christian-perspectives-on-animal-rights.html. Accessed 17 May 2016.
17. John Berkman, "Toward a Thomistic Theology of Animality," https://www.academia.edu/3183357/Towards_a_Thomistic_Theology_of_Animality_2009.
18. Jean Porter, "A Thomistic Interpretation of Moral Emotions in Human and Non-Human Animals," *Journal of Moral Theology* (3)2 June 2014.
19. John Berkman, "From Theological Speciesm to a Theological Ethology: Where Catholic Moral Theology Needs to Go," *Journal of Moral Theology* (3) 2 June 2014.
20. http://www.peta.org/features/pope-benedict-xvi/. Accessed May 17, 2016.
21. *United Press International*, "Pope Urges Respect for Animals," October 3, 1982.
22. Pope Francis, *Laudato Si'*, http://w2.vatican.va/content/francesco/en/encyclicals/documents/papa-francesco_20150524_enciclica-laudato-si.html #11. Accessed May 17, 2016.
23. Ibid., #138
24. "A good part of our genetic code is shared by many living beings." Ibid, 138.
25. *Laudato Si'*, #33
26. Ibid., #34
27. Ibid., #67
28. Ibid., #140
29. Ibid., #241
30. http://www.nydailynews.com/opinion/bruce-friedrich-pope-clear-animals-heaven-article-1.2302320
31. *Laudato Si'*, #243
32. Ibid., #130
33. Ibid.
34. Ibid., #145
35. Ibid., #129
36. I had a spirited debate on this very topic with Christopher Tollefsen, http://

catholicmoraltheology.com/justice-and-animals-a-brief-reply-to-christopher-tollefsen/. Accessed May 17, 2016.
37. *Laudato Si'*, #67
38. Ibid., #66
39. http://www.humanesociety.org/news/press_releases/2013/05/horrible-100-puppy-mill-report-050913.html. Accessed May 17, 2016.
40. Charles Camosy, "The Use of Animals in Biomedical Research—Can Moral Theology Fill the Gap?" *Journal of Moral Theology* (3)2 June 2014.

ANTHROPOCENTRISM AND INTEGRAL ECOLOGY IN GERMAIN GRISEZ'S NATURAL LAW

Jacaranda Turvey Tait

INTRODUCTION

Anthropocentrism in Catholic social teaching, with its emphasis on the dignity of the human person as *imago Dei*, has been widely regarded as a stumbling block in the path of progress towards what has been called the "greening of the papacy."[1] The aim of this paper is to ask whether Grisez's natural law has been accurately characterized as anthropocentric, to what extent it anticipates developments in the papal encyclical *Laudato Si'*, and how it might be applied to the climate challenge. Highlighting discords within Catholic teaching on animal rights, I ask how the pivotal position of human dignity might be retained, given the emphasis on valuing nature intrinsically in *Laudato Si'*. In pursuing this research it has been my hope that renewed attention to Grisez's environmentalism might challenge natural lawyers to engage with ecological issues and environmentalists to rethink their dismissal of natural law as a potential ally in their quest for sustainable solutions to our contemporary ecological crisis.

In this paper I shall argue that Grisez presents a broad view of human flourishing: to dismiss his natural law as perniciously "anthropocentric" is to overlook this and hence to undervalue his contribution to ecological ethics. Arguing that Grisez anticipates the emergence of "integral ecology" as an expression of the indivisibility of human and natural ecology in *Laudato Si'*, I shall apply Grisez's thought to the climate challenge, contending that his insights provide a helpful perspective on some central principles of climate justice and help flesh out the current Catholic ethical position on issues including global governance, divestment, and carbon trading. I shall argue that incongruities in Grisez's position on animal rights, reflecting those in current Catholic teaching, might be resolved either by employing an alternative rights construction or by extending neighbor-love to nature. Finally, I shall argue that construction of the *imago Dei* as "responsible relationship" coheres with Grisez's natural law and with Vatican teaching on the *imago Dei* and human environmental responsibility.

ANTHROPOCENTRISM

With the emergence of the ecological crisis as a "sign of the times," it has been argued that Catholic teaching is evolving, adapting the principles of the common good tradition to meet this new challenge. William French sees a progressive "greening" of recent papal thought since the publication in 1987 of *Sollicitudo rei socialis*, the first encyclical to give sustained attention to ecological issues.[2] Donal Dorr sees an "option for the poor and the earth" unfolding as the central principle of Catholic teaching, although he laments the fact that Pope Benedict XVI did not locate his teaching on the economic crisis within the larger context of a new ecological paradigm,[3] arguing that the teaching remains recalcitrantly anthropocentric.[4] Jame Schaefer calls for the development of the common good tradition towards a new "earth solidarity" and away from a human-centered orientation that values nature only instrumentally. These and many other voices in ecotheology call for a radical re-centering of Catholic social teaching in response to the ecological crisis.

In contrast, Germain Grisez adopts a conscientiously orthodox dialectical methodology: theology is always subordinate and never superior to the normative expressions of the Church's faith. He holds to the inerrancy of Holy Scripture[6] and the infallibility of the teaching office of the Church, in matters of faith and morality, as heir to the apostolic tradition.[7] Hence, it is no surprise that his ethics are dismissed by environmentalist critics as ecologically inhospitable: this critique exactly parallels the dissatisfaction with

Vatican teaching expressed by ecotheologians. For Michael Northcott, Grisez's ethics are merely "a restatement of classic Christian anthropocentrism," overemphasizing the Dominion motif and offering "weak moral grounds" for valuing nature independently of human needs.[8] Similarly, legal scholars Bebhinn Donnelly and Patrick Bishop contend that "in the new natural law scheme we are not afforded the opportunity to ask whether there can be a reason for action not connected to what is good for human beings." In their view the "classical natural law formulation" is a more promising source of an ecocentric ethics, upholding a vision of human fulfilment that cannot be realized by advancing only those capabilities that secure a benefit for us.[9] In order to examine the extent to which such critiques are valid, a brief exposition of Grisez's thought on mission and vocation, work, nature, and property and how these topics are interrelated is required, to which task we now turn.

For Grisez, personal vocation is the central organizing principle in the life of the faithful.[10] Each Christian—lay or ordained—is called to a unique task through which (s)he participates in the collective mission of the Church. However vocation is not to be understood narrowly or individualistically: extending to "the whole of life, including such matters as friendships and legitimate recreation, it specifies all the individual and social responsibilities of a Christian."[11] The concept of vocation functions within the Grisez-Finnis system much like John Rawls's idea that each person should adopt a "rational plan of life"[12]: rather than altering our moral responsibilities, it orders our pursuit of the good as a personal response to God's love. Indeed, logically, to avoid the narrowness Grisez cautions against, our vocation must embrace ecological as well as social responsibilities, which Pope John Paul II tells us are an essential part of faith,[13] and work as well as recreation. Grisez has a high view of work as a basic human good: through work, people develop their skills, actualize their potential, and realize themselves as moral agents.[14] Good work, for Grisez, uses nature to serve human needs within the framework of God's plan[15] and we wield God-given authority to that end alone. There is no license to exploit or destroy in the Dominion mandate as Grisez understands it:[16] we are called to socially and ecologically responsible work as our share in the Divine activity of creation and redemption.[17]

Natural entities are neither to be exploited nor to be held sacred,[18] but may be used for good human purposes within the limits set by a deep respect for creation and the Creator.[19] Good human use of non-human creatures, Grisez tells us, accords with the direction of practical reason and fulfills rather than conflicts with the creature's inherent meaning and value.[20] Humans are responsible to God and to each other—not least to future generations—for the use we make of God's gift of nature, which in effect we hold on trust for our descendants as the common patrimony of humankind.[21]

Grisez proscribes restraint and reasonableness as the hallmarks of appropriate human use of creation, condemning unrestricted, exploitative "development" which leads to irreversible changes in the natural world, depletes natural resources and perpetuates injustice to the poor.[22] For Grisez, our sins—specifically laziness, abuse of our God-given dominion and pursuit of pleasure, wealth, status, power, and the illusion of security—are the root causes of ecological devastation.[23] He especially condemns powerful people and property owners who "decide what will count as fair and even who will count as persons,"[24] engaging in wanton waste and despoliation of the earth whilst pursuing, at best, the long-term interests of themselves and those they care for rather than the common good.[25]

For Grisez, "people's occupancy of places and uses of things, together with the requirement of fairness, cause [...] things to become property, that is, to be morally tied in a special way to a particular person, family, or other community."[26] However, since wealth and material objects are not goods intrinsic to human persons there is no absolute right to ownership: property is always held subject to the universal destination of goods and the strict obligation in justice to aid the destitute.[27] Possession does not license irresponsible use nor is property accumulation justified beyond that which is needed for the pursuit of one's vocation.[28] Private assets are to be shared, conserved, and used responsibly for the common good.

Unlike Rawls's "thin" conception of the public good, which attempts a neutral stance towards differing comprehensive doctrines of the good life, the new natural law centers on a theologically and ecologically "thick" conception of human flourishing.[29] For Grisez the moral life is focused not on the satisfaction of human desires or preferences but on the eschatological attainment of right relationship with God, our fellow humans, and creation. Thus, although there is an anthropocentric thread running through Grisez's moral theology, this intertwines with theocentric and eco-inclusive strands to weave a worldview that is colored throughout with ecological sensitivity.

Although Grisez's natural law does not include "harmony with the natural world" as a separate dimension of human flourishing, its pursuit is intelligible as intrinsic to work and recreation, aesthetic appreciation, and especially communion with God as the source of meaning and value. Nevertheless, Sabina Alkire argues that harmony with nature is not reducible to other dimensions of flourishing and that this is an omission the Grisez School would do well to correct.[30] Perhaps more controversially, Rufus Black suggests that recognition of this dimension "is only possible for those with some sort of 'religious' belief who understand the world as an expression of the more-than-human."[31] On Black's view, Grisez's present account seems in danger of reducing his environmental ethics to a species of "divine command" theory. Thus this aspect of Grisez's work is easily overlooked by legal scholars focused on his secular natural law.

It seems to me that there is nothing in Donnelly and Bishop's preferred construction of human fulfillment that the Grisez School would find objectionable or outside the bounds of their own conception of the moral life. While in the new natural law scheme practical reason requires and can only provide justification for action in pursuit of human goods, Grisez nonetheless argues for kindness to sentient animals on the basis of their capacity for suffering, with no necessary human advantage in view,[32] and he advocates human action to provide for harmless creatures and to protect biodiversity.[33] The apparent contradiction is resolved through Grisez's inclusive, theological construction of our flourishing as social animals in dependent relationships with the ecosystem and with God who loves all his creatures and calls us to care for his world.

INTEGRAL ECOLOGY

As we have seen, for Grisez, kindness towards other creatures is not precluded by the central importance of human dignity: indeed authentic development of human potential requires attention to sustainability. Grisez, like Celia Deane-Drummond,[34] does not make the unduly sharp distinction between human and natural ecology that Donal Dorr finds problematic in *Centesimus annus*.[35] In *Laudato Si'*, the new motif of "integral ecology,"[36] with its echoes of "integral human development" from *Populorum Progressio*, clarifies the essential unity of human and natural ecology. On my reading, Grisez's natural law is integrally ecological, although he does not use the term, whether one sees this as a new conceptual development in Catholic social teaching, which he anticipates, or simply a clarification, in *Laudato Si'*, of earlier ambiguous teaching. As we have seen, Grisez weaves into his moral system an appreciation of nature's inherent value, stressing God's declaration that his pre-human creation was good.[37] Since his dialectical methodology seeks to expound and organize Catholic teaching rather than to advocate theological innovation,[38] it seems clear that Grisez himself understood inherent value as Catholic orthodoxy before Pope Francis made this explicit.[39]

John Paul II distinguishes between proper exercise of dominion and "anthropological error" in which humankind "discovers its capacity to transform and in a certain sense create the world through its own work [and] forgets that this is always based on God's prior and original gift of the things that are."[40] Environmentalist critiques of the centrality of the *imago Dei* in Christian theology overlook this important distinction and, focusing narrowly on its ecological implications, disregard the importance of the *imago Dei* in social ethics. Yet the central Christian narrative, from Herod's slaughter of the infants to Christ's crucifixion, forms us as a people with staunch respect for human dignity and implacable moral outrage wherever the innocent are tortured or killed. If the Church is to evolve a stronger focus on the environment in the light of the ecological crisis, it cannot be at the expense of this central truth of faith, which loss seems to be the chief fear of those who resist the proposed paradigm shift to ecocentrism. An ethic of integral ecology resists such problematic ecological egalitarianism while clarifying the natural boundaries within which integral human development is to be promoted and pursued.

LAUDATO SI' AND CLIMATE CHANGE

In keeping with the tradition of its genre, *Laudato Si'* is an essay in moral theology in the light of papal discernment. As Robert George has pointed out,[41] the Pope's teaching authority does not extend to scientific questions, a limitation acknowledged in the encyclical.[42] Nevertheless, lamenting the fact that some committed and prayerful Christians still tend to ridicule environmental concern,[43] Pope Francis states baldly that "a frank look at the facts" confirms the dilapidation of our common home,[44] and *Laudato Si'* acknowledges "a very solid scientific consensus" indicating that we are presently causing and witnessing "a disturbing warming of the climate system."[45] For Pope Francis, the ecological crisis is now an issue of such grave concern that "doomsday predictions can no longer be dismissed with irony or disdain."[46]

The Catholic Church has long acknowledged the problems of atmospheric pollution and climate change. In *Laudato Si'*, Pope Francis addresses food security, access to fresh water, and biodiversity loss linked to global warming, aiming to present a clear articulation of the Church's position, initiate an inclusive conversation,[47] promote open and honest debate,[48] and stimulate concerted action to mitigate the climate threat. Reiterating established Catholic teaching on water as a human right,[49] and noting links between climate and scarcity especially in Africa where crop yields are already threatened by drought and rising temperatures,[50] *Laudato Si'* stresses the grave social debt owed to those suffering from water poverty, which prevents them from living lives commensurate with their dignity.[51] Pope Francis clearly feels the loss of biodiversity in an acutely personal way, lamenting especially the decline in marine species that is "turning the wonderworld of the seas into an underwater cemetery bereft of color and life,"[52] a phrase that seems prophetic in the light of the current mass bleaching event affecting almost all of the Great Barrier Reef as the underlying upward trend in global temperatures combines with *el Niño* to devastating effect.[53]

Pope Francis attributes our inadequate collective efforts to address this crisis to moral and cultural failure, criticising ecologically deficient economic models that do not weigh intergenerational justice and ecosystem services appropriately,[54] and highlighting failures of governance at every level. The lack of global institutions means that international relations are dominated and obstructed by assertions of self-interest by competing nation states instead of being guided by a joint commitment to the global common good.[55] In some countries, weak structures, corruption, or the collapse of the rule of law undermines confidence that environmental legislation will be enforced.[56] Yet even where robust institutions exist, campaigns of misinformation, evasion of responsibility, and political short-termism have resulted in slow progress towards climate solutions.[57]

Laudato Si' advocates a global treaty incorporating the precautionary[58] and polluter-pays[59] principles as well as intergenerational justice and fair burden-sharing. The Paris agreement, although it was an important landmark, fell far short of its own ideals as well as those of the Catholic Church. Locally, Pope Francis commends civic support for small-scale production,[60] although he does not specifically challenge the morality and climate consequences of factory farming.[61] He stresses the importance of moral and aesthetic education as essential to building the culture and character needed to face the challenges ahead[62] and commends social and environmental entrepreneurship. Reiterating the calls of his predecessors for "ecological conversion" including individual lifestyle change, Pope Francis recommends effectuating consumer power to support sustainable choices.[63] Some commentators suggest *Laudato Si'* will generate more pressure for fossil-fuel divestment, although the issue is not directly addressed.[64]

As Daniel Scheid notes, the encyclical is realistic about our ecological predicament, yet its message remains profoundly hopeful,[65] insisting that love always proves more powerful than the forces of violence and disintegration, even in dire circumstances.[66] Hence gestures of generosity, solidarity, and care cannot but well up in us, since we were made for love.[67] The potential to make a positive contribution to building a "civilization of love"[68] with the capacity and resilience to protect human dignity and the environment exists in every human heart. This gives us reason to hope that our generation will be remembered for generously shouldering our responsibilities,[69] for the awakening of a new reverence for life, the firm resolve to achieve sustainability, the quickening of the struggle for justice and peace, and the joyful celebration of life.[70]

There is much theological work to be done in analyzing *Laudato Si'* and making its message more widely accessible. This paper seeks to contribute a Grisez School perspective to that larger intellectual endeavor. In a number of areas, insights gleaned from Grisez's environmental ethics can clarify the meaning of the text and illuminate the path to understanding and applying Catholic teaching on the environment as articulated in *Laudato Si'*.

GRISEZ, CLIMATE CHANGE, AND *LAUDATO SI'*

Climate change has been described as "the ultimate global commons problem."[71] Such problems lead to a risk of overexploitation of the commons—in this case the planetary atmosphere—as uncoordinated parties pursue their self-interest. In this context, Pope Francis calls for a true world political authority.[72] Catholic teaching on supranational institutions is generally unpopular with conservatives, but Grisez helpfully explains the thinking behind it:

> Since there is a universal common good, the good of humankind as a whole, which neither national governments nor existing organizations adequately serve, Catholics should support the self-limitation of sovereignty on behalf of their nation and its collaboration in developing a worldwide political authority capable of discerning and evaluating problems which affect the universal common good and effectively

directing international cooperation towards their just resolution. Pending the development of such an authority, Catholics should support the participation of their government in existing international organizations to the extent the activities of the latter seem to serve the universal common good.[73]

In the absence of global governance, international cooperation to protect the global commons requires negotiations in fora such as the annual conferences of the parties to the UNFCCC. Pope Francis urges action towards a treaty to impose abatement obligations.[74] It has been argued that the only way to ensure broad participation in a climate treaty is to build into its design a requirement of International Paretianism: individual nation states must be better off under the treaty, with side payments made to less climate-vulnerable parties to induce their participation.[75] Pragmatism might counsel such an approach, given the Hobbesian state-of-nature that pertains in the international arena, but, on my reading, neither Grisez nor Pope Francis would recognize such an outcome as "climate justice."

Grisez is clear that justice requires differential burden-sharing in mitigating environmental harms:

> Because poor individuals and societies have fewer alternatives, they may rightly accept side effects wrong for the wealthy to accept. Thus the affluent should willingly accept greater burdens in preventing and correcting pollution, rather than favoring measures which overburden the poor by imposing identical burdens on rich and poor alike.[76]

Although carbon pollution is not specifically mentioned, the general principle Grisez articulates is clearly relevant, echoing the concept of "common but differentiated responsibilities and capabilities" expressed in the UNFCCC[77] and in the Rio Declaration.[78] Clearly, as time goes on and emissions continue to rise, the available headroom for prioritizing the development needs of the poor envisioned in the framework convention is increasingly exhausted, forcing a situation in which environmentally acceptable outcomes will require rapid abatement action from all major emitters, including China, India, Brazil, and South Africa. The challenge is to design fair abatement curves and mechanisms for compensating poor countries who invest in mitigation measures that would otherwise compromise their poverty-reduction strategies.

For Grisez, the universal destination of goods confers an absolute Christian duty to assist the destitute, which is all the more urgent where there has been an historical injustice, since "needs due to some defect of a community to which one belongs [...] deserve special consideration even if in no way one's own fault."[79] Again, Grisez does not specifically invoke the problem of historical emissions responsibility, but the concept he elucidates is clearly applicable. Posner and Weisbach argue that no allowance should be made for "carbon debt" in designing a "just" treaty, since today's Americans cannot be held responsible for the actions of past generations, and U.S. failure to cooperate with international abatement efforts did not amount to negligence.[80] In contrast, a Catholic concept of climate justice would need to incorporate some mechanism to account for historical emissions disparities.

In an unusually specific policy intervention, *Laudato Si'* is critical of carbon trading, a point that David Cloutier seems to overlook.[81] Interestingly, Posner and Weisbach favor a carbon tax regime over cap-and-trade, arguing that per-capita allocation of permits would result in enormous redistribution of wealth from industrialized to developing nations, effectively dooming the climate negotiations.[82] Yet Michael Northcott is scathing about carbon trading for quite different reasons, seeing such market mechanisms as "a highly ambiguous development" that has created tremendous new trading opportunities and new opportunities for fraud and injustice while failing to incentivize real reductions in emissions.[83]

The thinking behind Pope Francis's objection to carbon trading is unclear and here the lens of the new natural law does not bring it into sharp focus. However some tentative conclusions can be drawn: for Grisez, the universal destination of goods does not imply "a basic or *prima facie* claim on the part of each individual to an equal portion of the world's goods,"[84] which suggests that convergence towards equal per-capita emissions allowances is not essential to a Grisez School concept of climate justice. On the other hand, his argument concerning the right of the state to expropriate property that is being used irresponsibly[85] suggests that he might oppose the grandfathering of permits to existing polluters. Pope Francis's summary dismissal of carbon trading is troubling: such schemes have their able defenders,[86] and it is not clear that they are either necessarily inadequate as a policy instrument or simply an immoral ploy to maintain excessive consumption. Effectiveness would depend on setting a high enough carbon price—ratcheting it up over time to drive emissions down—and the unfair advantaging of current polluters would only apply to the grandfathering of emissions rights and not to per-capita allocation schemes or auctioning of permits.

Some commentators have suggested that *Laudato Si'* endorses a left-wing anti-market agenda, but this interpretation of the encyclical seems at odds with its commendation of various models of enterprise and economic activity.[87] Business directed to producing wealth and improving our world is held up as a noble vocation and a fruitful source of prosperity, especially where it sees the creation of worthwhile employment as an essential part of its service to the common good. This is in line with Grisez's position that some are called to administer material things for the general benefit:

> Sometimes, although its owners could give away property or money, they have such a gift for administering material goods that they should accept that as an element of their personal vocation. For example, people with both surplus wealth and skill in management can rightly set up or invest in businesses which provide just wages for gainful work and useful goods and services at fair prices, along with enough profit to compensate them reasonably for their work which contributes to society's common good.[88]

Those who have the good fortune to have capital to invest, Grisez argues, should "try to avoid turning over the management of [their] savings to people who will use them in unjust or otherwise immoral activities," instead choosing ethical investment opportunities.[89] When we consider fossil-fuel investments we should try to discern whether or not this effectively supports immoral activity in the light of climate change. *Laudato Si'*, as we have seen, is silent on the issue of divestment, leaving such decisions to the individual conscience. The issue is by no means clear cut since use of oil and gas needs to be phased out and we are all complicit in countless ways in the fossil-fuelled economy. Anthony Giddens warns against the easy demonization of carbon-intensive industries, noting that BP publically acknowledged the climate threat in 1997.[90] Other oil companies rapidly followed suit.[91] As Giddens says, "a new generation of business leaders [...] is arising which not only acknowledges the perils of climate change, but is active in the vanguard of reaction to it."[92] Switching investments towards green alternatives is one way in which conscientious Catholics might act to accelerate the transition to climate security. Alternatively Catholic shareholders could exert pressure on oil companies to refocus their activities towards future energies.

Responding to *Laudato Si'*, parishes and families can be active change agents in their communities. For Grisez, the practice of conservation is no "merely fashionable cause"[93] but an essential aspect of the Christian moral life. He connects sinful profligacy with environmental damage, underscoring that the harm done to others by living a wasteful consumerist lifestyle can no longer be judged insignificant, given what we now know about the environmental impact of such choices.[94] Grisez expounds and Pope Francis reiterates established Catholic teaching on the importance of a temperate lifestyle. The lack of public support for sustained lifestyle change[95] is a major stumbling block to achieving the necessary carbon cuts: for example, modeling studies on emissions reductions achievable through technological greening of the vehicle fleet suggest that targets will not be met without a significant behavior-change contribution to the transition project.[96] Catholic action in response to *Laudato Si'* has the potential to stimulate mass public engagement in the global transition project.

ANIMAL RIGHTS

Grisez shares Pope Francis's concern for biodiversity and constructs a duty of compassion towards animals,[97] although he does not see them as bearers of rights.[98] The "theory of rights presupposed by most animal rights proponents"—Grisez tells us—"implies that, while any mature and normal mammal has rights, unborn and newborn human individuals have none whatsoever." He goes on to assert that animal rights advocates reject the Christian view of persons and that all rights theories have more in common with each other than with the Christian worldview.[99] He appears to treat Peter Singer's preference for utilitarianism as the paradigm of rights construction, which is problematic not least because Singer—on his own account—does not advocate "animal rights" as such.[100] Furthermore, since the moral protection Singer sees as appropriate for other sentient non-persons applies equally to humans who do not meet his criteria for personhood, Grisez's statement is not true even for Singer himself. Tom Regan counters a similar objection to that raised by Grisez: his rights theory does not make being the subject-of-a-life a necessary condition for inherent value, he leaves the empirical question as to whether unborn children and infants are subjects-of-a-life unresolved, and—like Singer—he does not strip hypothetical human non-persons of all moral protection.[101]

Grisez's treatment of animal ethics remains speciesist, notwithstanding his endorsement of inherent value and the integral ecology that pervades his natural law ethics: animals may be used to serve the basic good of persons. This includes "killing them, harming them and/or inflicting pain on them to the extent either necessary for the purpose or unavoidable without imposing significant burdens on human beings."[102] Grisez's recognition of inherent value in non-human animals and his treatment of cruelty seem discordant, implying that it is *not cruel* to deliberately cause suffering to a sentient being as long as some tangible benefit to science or medicine is in prospect, although it has long been seen as unacceptable to inflict pain "needlessly."[103] This reflects an anthropocentric residue in Catholic social teaching which is thrown into sharper relief with the endorsement of inherent value in *Laudato Si'*. Are we to regard the production of cheap meat as a human benefit sufficient to outweigh cruelty to factory-farmed livestock? Grisez suggests such practices should be reformed;[104] yet on what basis are we to distinguish this conceptually from animal suffering in medical experimentation? In both cases non-human goods are subordinated to human goods.

NEIGHBORS TO NATURE?

Marcus Mescher[105] and Daniel Miller[106] argue that the Good Samaritan narrative can teach us to be neighbors to nature. For Mescher, while relationships with non-human animals cannot be fully reciprocal, since they cannot be moral subjects with duties comparable to our own, *agape* love can be unidirectional; hence, although ecological responsibility is not explicitly addressed in the parable, "it still may serve to inspire disciples to 'go and do likewise' in a way that honors our responsibility to our non-human covenant partners." He proposes that we should love nature in a different mode from our love for fellow humans: to be a loving neighbor to non-human creation would be shaped by respect and responsibility consonant with the unique ability we have to care for the rest of creation.[107] This move allows Mescher to maintain the ontological distinction between *Homo sapiens* as *imago Dei* and other species whilst denying any license to exploit nature; anthropocentrism is replaced with a theocentric faithfulness to God's desire for all creation. In a similar vein, as Deborah Jones notes,[108] much of Grisez's creation theology, with its emphasis on our duty of kindness towards animals and restraint in our use of natural resources, coheres with a theocentric worldview.

Miller's adoption of Emil Brunner's construction of human uniqueness as "spiritual-responsible (*geistigverantwortlichen*) relational being"[109] parallels post-Vatican II recovery of the *imago Dei* in Catholic theology: the International Theological Commission has sought to reaffirm the truth that human persons are created in the image of God as relational beings in order to enjoy personal communion with God and with one another and to exercise responsible stewardship of the created world. Human beings exercise this stewardship by gaining scientific understanding, by caring responsibly for animals and the environment, and by guarding their own biological integrity.[110] Neighbor-love, as Miller argues, goes beyond the resource-management implied by "stewardship,"[111] yet it is clear that such love need not entail the collapse of the ontological distinctiveness of the human person.

CONCLUSION

This paper contends that although Grisez's natural law is at times anthropocentric, we should not overlook the theocentric and bio-inclusive facets of his thought. His ethics are more open to environmental engagement than either his disciples or his critics have allowed, opening up the possibility of constructing a Grisez School response to contemporary moral problems such as climate justice and animal rights. As we have seen, Grisez embraces the idea of inherent value in nature and anticipates the emergence of "integral ecology" as a descriptor of the Catholic moral life. Grisez's thought on global governance, conservation, and collective responsibility helps us to construct a Catholic concept of climate justice and to question the ethics of current carbon mitigation pledges. A tension in Grisez's animal ethics, which remains anthropocentric, leaves unresolved questions. However, through the lens of the Good Samaritan, human dignity as *imago Dei* comes into focus as a call to responsible relationship. Such a move coheres with Grisez's environmental ethics and with Catholic thought on the *imago Dei* as simultaneous communion and stewardship, pointing the way to a consistently humane animal ethics. This suggests possibilities for post-*Laudato Si'* development of Catholic doctrine beyond anthropocentrism without jeopardizing the unique moral standing of vulnerable persons: rather than undergoing a paradigm shift it seems likely that Catholic doctrine will continue to evolve incrementally, as the whole Church reflects on the signs of the times in the light of immutable principles of the faith. Close attention to Grisez's environmental ethics illuminates Catholic teaching on the environment and its possible future trajectory. Grisez exhorts Christians today to "make a special effort to bring the light of faith to bear in understanding their responsibilities for subhuman creation."[112] The climate challenge as a "sign of the times" makes this task of faithful theological reflection all the more urgent.

Acknowledgments: Thanks are due to David Clough and Celia Deane-Drummond for their supervision of the doctoral project on which this paper is based and to an anonymous reviewer for constructive criticism of an earlier draft.

NOTES

1. Ronald A. Simkins and John J. O'Keefe (eds.) "The Greening of the Papacy," *Journal of Religion and Society,* Supplement 9 (2013). http://moses.creighton.edu/jrs/toc/SS09.html. Accessed 24 May 2016.
2. William French, "Catholicism and the Common Good of the Biosphere" in *An Ecology of the Spirit: Religious Reflections and Environmental Consciousness* edited by Michael Horace Barnes (Lanham, M.D: University Press of America, 1994), 185–186.
3. Donal Dorr, *Option for the Poor and the Earth: Catholic Social Teaching* (Maryknoll NY: Orbis Books, 2012), 431.
4. Dorr, *Option for the Poor and the Earth*, 438.
5. Jame Schaefer, "Solidarity, Subsidiarity and Preference for the Poor: Extending Catholic Social Teaching in Response to the Climate Crisis" in *Confronting the Climate Crisis: Catholic Theological Perspectives* edited by Jame Schaefer (Milwaukee, WI: Marquette University Press, 2011) 389–425, 411.
6. Germain Grisez, *The Way of the Lord Jesus,* Volume 1, *Christian Moral Principles*, (Chicago: Franciscan Herald Press, 1983) Chapter 35, QB (3) 836.
7. Grisez, *Christian Moral Principles*, Chapter 35, QA (12) 833.
8. Michael Northcott, "The Moral Standing of Nature and the New Natural Law," in *The Revival of Natural Law: Philosophical, Theological and Ethical Responses to the Finnis-Grisez School*, edited by Nigel Biggar and Rufus Black (Aldershot: Ashgate, 2000) 262–281, 268.
9. Bebhinn Donnelly and Patrick Bishop "Natural Law and Ecocentrism," *Journal of Environmental Law*, 19.1 (2007) 89–101.
10. Grisez, *Christian Moral Principles*, Chapter 28, QE, 693.
11. Germain Grisez, *The Way of the Lord Jesus, Volume 2, Living a Christian Life,* (Quincy, Illinois: Franciscan Press, 1993) Chapter 10 QE2 (b) 804.
12. John Finnis, *Natural Law and Natural Rights* (Oxford: Clarendon Press, 1987) 103.
13. John Paul II, "Peace with the Creator God, Peace with all Creation": *Message for the World Day of Peace* 1990, no. 15. https://w2.vatican.va/content/john-paul-ii/en/messages/peace/documents/hf_jp-ii_mes_19891208_xxiii-world-day-for-peace.html. Accessed 24 May 2016.

14. Grisez, *Christian Moral Principles*, Chapter 5 QD 11, 124. See also Grisez, *Living a Christian Life*, Chapter 10, QA1(a) 756.
15. Grisez, *Living a Christian Life*, Chapter 10, QB2(e) 777.
16. Ibid., QB2(b) 775.
17. Ibid., QB1(c) 774; QB3(d) 780.
18. Ibid., QB1(a) and (b) 772–773.
19. Ibid., QB4(a) and (b) 780–781.
20. Ibid., QB3(a) 778.
21. Ibid., QB2(c) 776 n. 40.
22. Ibid., QB1(a) 772.
23. Ibid., QB4(c) 781.
24. Ibid., QB1(a) 773.
25. Ibid., QB1(a) 772.
26. Ibid., QD1 789.
27. Ibid., QE1(a) 800; QD1(d) 791; See also John Finnis, *Aquinas: Moral, Political and Legal Theory* (Oxford: OUP, 1998), 188–196.
28. Ibid., QE2(b) 804.
29. John Finnis, *Natural Law and Natural Rights*, 106.
30. Sabina Alkire, "The Basic Dimensions of Human Flourishing: A Comparison of Accounts" in: Biggar & Black (eds.) *The Revival of Natural Law* 73–110, 98.
31. Rufus Black, *Christian Moral Realism, Natural Law, Narrative, Virtue and the Gospel* (Oxford: OUP, 2000), 135.
32. Grisez, *Living a Christian Life*, Chapter 10, QC2(a) 785.
33. Ibid. QC2(b) 786.
34. Celia Deane-Drummond, "Joining in the Dance: Catholic Social Teaching and Ecology," *New Blackfriars* 93.1044 (March 2012) 193–212, p. 202, 205.
35. Dorr, *Option for the Poor and the Earth*, 422.
36. Pope Francis, *Laudato Si': On Care for our Common Home* (London: Catholic Truth Society, 2015), 10–11. http://w2.vatican.va/content/francesco/en/encyclicals/documents/papa-francesco_20150524_enciclica-laudato-si.html. Accessed 30 May 2016.
37. Grisez, *Living a Christian Life*, Chapter 10, QB1 772.
38. Grisez, *Christian Moral Principles*, Chapter 1 QC 1 7.
39. *Laudato Si'* 36, 69, 76, 140.
40. Grisez, *Living a Christian Life*, Chapter 10, QB1(a) n. 30 772–773.
41. Robert P. George, "Four Things to Remember About the Pope's Environment Letter," *First Things*, 1 March 2015. http://www.firstthings.com/blogs/firstthoughts/2015/01/four-things-to-remember-about-the-popes-environment-letter. Accessed 24 May 2016.
42. *Laudato Si'* 188.
43. *Laudato Si'* 217.

44. *Laudato Si'* 61.
45. *Laudato Si'* 23.
46. *Laudato Si'* 161.
47. *Laudato Si'* 14.
48. *Laudato Si'* 188.
49. Pontifical Council for Justice and Peace, *Compendium of the Social Doctrine of the Church,* 365, 447, 485.
50. *Laudato Si'* 51.
51. *Laudato Si'* 30.
52. *Laudato Si'* 41.
53. Michael Slezak, "Great Barrier Reef Bleaching Made 175 Times More Likely By Human-caused Climate Change, Say Scientists," *The Guardian*, Thursday 28 April 2016. http://www.theguardian.com/environment/2016/apr/29/great-barrier-reef-bleaching-made-175-times-likelier-by-human-caused-climate-change-say-scientists. Accessed 25 May 2016.
54. *Laudato Si'* 190.
55. *Laudato Si'* 169.
56. *Laudato Si'* 142.
57. *Laudato Si'* 26; 169; 178.
58. *Laudato Si'* 186.
59. *Laudato Si'* 167.
60. *Laudato Si'* 129.
61. Charles Camosy, "*Laudato Si'* On Non-human Animals: Three Hopeful Signs, Three Missed Opportunities," *Catholic Moral Theology*, 24 June 2015. http://catholicmoraltheology.com/laudato-si-on-non-human-animals-three-hopeful-signs-three-missed-opportunities/. Accessed 25 May 2016.
62. *Laudato Si'* 215.
63. *Laudato Si'* 206.
64. John Schwartz, "Papal Encyclical Makes Proponents of Fossil Fuel Divestment Happy," *Crux*, 18 June 2015. http://www.cruxnow.com/church/2015/06/18/papal-encyclical-makes-propnents-of-fossil-fuel-divestment-happy/. Accessed 25 May 2016.
65. Daniel P. Scheid, "*Laudato Si'*: Appealing to Our Better Natures," *Political Theology*, 19 June 2015. http://www.politicaltheology.com/blog/laudato-si-appealing-to-our-better-natures-daniel-p-scheid/. Accessed 25 May 2016.
66. *Laudato Si'* 149.
67. *Laudato Si'* 58.
68. *Laudato Si'* 231.
69. *Laudato Si'* 165.
70. *Laudato Si'* 207.
71. Joseph E. Aldy and Robert N. Stavins, "Introduction: International Policy Architecture for Global Climate Change" in *Architectures for Agreement: Addressing Global Climate Change in the Post-Kyoto World,* edited by

Joseph E. Aldy and Robert N. Stavins (New York: Cambridge University Press, 2007), 1.
72. *Laudato Si'* 175.
73. Grisez, *Living a Christian Life*, Chapter 11, QC2(f) 868.
74. *Laudato Si'* 173.
75. Eric A. Posner and David Weisbach, *Climate Change Justice* (Princeton, NJ: Princeton University Press, 2010), 6, 179.
76. Grisez, *Living a Christian Life*, Chapter 10, QE5(i) 815.
77. United Nations Framework Convention on Climate Change, 1992, Article 3.1 https://unfccc.int/resource/docs/convkp/conveng.pdf. Accessed 26 May 2016.
78. *Rio Declaration on Environment and Development*, 1992, Principle 7 http://www.unep.org/documents.multilingual/default.asp?documentid=78&articleid=1163. Accessed 26 May 2016.
79. Grisez, *Living a Christian Life*, Chapter 10, QE5(c) 812.
80. Posner and Weisbach, *Climate Change Justice*, p. 113–114, 190.
81. David Cloutier, *Reading, Praying, Living Pope Francis's* Laudato Si' (Collegeville, Minnesota: Liturgical Press, 2015), 65.
82. Ibid., 122.
83. Michael Northcott, *A Moral Climate: The Ethics of Global Warming* (London: Darton, Longman and Todd, 2007), 136.
84. Grisez, *Living a Christian Life*, Chapter 10, QD1(b) 790.
85. Grisez, *Living a Christian Life*, Chapter 10, QD2(e) and (f) 795.
86. See for example: Jeffrey Frankel, "Formulae for Quantitative Emissions Targets," pp. 31–56; Axel Michaelowa, "Graduation and deepening," 81–104, in: Aldy and Stavins, *Architectures for Agreement.*
87. Luigino Bruni, "*Laudato Si'* (Praise be to you) Is Far From Being Anti-business," Focolare, 26 June 2015. http://www.focolare.org/en/news/2015/06/26/enciclica-ed-economia-la-laudato-si-e-limpresa/. Accessed 26 May 2016.
88. Grisez, *Living a Christian Life*, Chapter 10, QE5(f) 814.
89. Ibid., QE6(e) 817.
90. Anthony Giddens, *The Politics of Climate Change* (Cambridge: Polity Press, 2009) 120.
91. Mark Moody-Stuart, Speech to the Carbon Trust Chairman's Dinner, Somerset House, London, 2 June 2015. https://www.carbontrust.com/news/2015/06/sir-mark-moody-stuart-speech-carbon-trust-chairmans-dinner. Accessed 26 May 2016.
92. Giddens, *The Politics of Climate Change*, 121.
93. Grisez, *Living a Christian Life*, Chapter 10, QE1(d) 803.
94. Ibid., QD4 799.
95. Giddens, *The Politics of Climate Change*, 101.
96. Steve Skippon, Supplementary Memorandum, Behaviour Change, House

of Lords Science and Technology Committee, 5 October 2010, 825. http://www.parliament.uk/documents/lords-committees/science-technology/behaviourchange/BCwrittenEvidenceStoZ.pdf. Accessed 30 May 2016.
97. Grisez, *Living a Christian Life*, Chapter 10, QC2(b), 786.
98. Ibid., QC1, 783.
99. Andrew Linzey's work is an obvious contemporaneous counter-example: Andrew Linzey, *Christianity and the Rights of Animals* (London, SPCK, 1987).
100. Peter Singer, *Animal Liberation*, second edition (London: Pimlico, 1995), 8.
101. Tom Regan, *The Case for Animal Rights* (Berkeley, CA: University of California Press, 1983), 319–320.
102. Grisez, *Living a Christian Life*, Chapter 10, QC2(c), 786–787.
103. *Catechism of the Catholic Church* (London: Geoffrey Chapman, 1994), 2418.
104. Grisez, *Living a Christian Life*, Chapter 10, 787 n. 54.
105. Marcus Mescher, "Neighbour to Nature," 200–217 in *Green Discipleship: Catholic Theological Ethics and the Environment*, edited by Tobias Winright (Winona, MN: Anselm Academic, 2011).
106. Daniel K. Miller, *Animal Ethics: The Lens of the Good Samaritan* (New York: Routledge, 2012).
107. Mescher, "Neighbour to Nature," 211.
108. Deborah M. Jones, *The School of Compassion: A Roman Catholic Theology of Animals* (Leominster: Gracewing, 2009), 267.
109. Miller, *Animal Ethics*, 33.
110. International Theological Commission, *Communion and Stewardship: Human Persons Created in the Image of God*, 2002. http://www.vatican.va/roman_curia/congregations/cfaith/cti_documents/rc_con_cfaith_doc_20040723_communion-stewardship_en.html. Accessed 26 May 2016.
111. Miller, *Animal Ethics*, 133.
112. Grisez, *Living a Christian Life*, Chapter 10, QB 2 (c), 776.

DOES NATURAL LAW DICTATE CARE FOR THE ENVIRONMENT SOLELY ON HUMAN-CENTERED GROUNDS?

By Marie George

It is commonly argued that natural law[1] dictates that human beings use the non-rational beings that are parts of the environment to sustain their lives; this type of argument goes back to Aristotle.[2] We have a natural inclination to live, and nature supplies us with the necessary means: plants, animals, and inanimate beings. In the words of Aquinas:

> [M]an has natural dominion over external things, because through reason and will he is able to use external things to his advantage, as they were made for him; for things that are less perfect are always for the sake of the more perfect.... And starting from this reason the Philosopher, in Bk. 1 of the *Politics*, proves that the possession of external things is natural to man.[3]

In addition, natural law dictates that our usage of these things be moderate, so as to be in keeping with our natural inclination to live, as immoderate usage can cause sickness and premature death. Natural law also dictates usage such that we do not deprive other humans of what they need to live, since the goods of the earth are naturally ordered to supplying the basic needs of all human individuals.[4] Are there, though, non-human-centered directives of natural law concerning how we should use non-rational creatures?

Drawing on the thought primarily of Aquinas and to some extent of Aristotle, I will argue that our natural inclinations are indicative of several non-human-centered directives concerning care of the environment. What I will present is more of a sketch than a fully reasoned-out position. Although I think all the notions I rely on here are defensible, I cannot defend them all in so short a space;

those who are familiar with Aquinas's thought will find my argumentation more compelling than those who are not. The first argument I will give is based on our natural inclination as specifically rational animals to know the truth, and thus to recognize the good as such, and consequently the goodness of non-rational beings. We are further able to assess what sort of love is the appropriate response to their goodness. Accordingly, natural law dictates that we show them this love. The second argument is based on the tendency we share with other substances, insofar as they are parts of a whole, to act in a manner that preserves the whole; accordingly, natural law dictates that we care for other species insofar as they contribute to the good of the universe. The third argument, like the first, is based on our natural inclination as specifically rational animals to know the truth, but in this case the truth concerning God, which includes the knowledge that non-rational beings are part of a universe meant to give glory to God. Consequently, we see that needlessly preventing them from doing so is contrary to natural law, as being contrary to the reverence we owe to God.

NATURAL LAW DICTATES THAT WE DO NOT DESTROY NON-RATIONAL NATURAL THINGS NEEDLESSLY BECAUSE OF THEIR INHERENT GOODNESS

It is proper to reason to know the good as such. While non-sentient natural things unconsciously seek their good, and while non-rational animals seek particular goods as useful or pleasant, rational beings are able to seek the good as such. Thus, Aquinas observes: "The will has for its object the good according to the notion of good; nature, however, does not attain to the common notion of good, but to this good which is its perfection."[5] We, as rational beings, by a certain age arrive at a vague notion of what goodness is. This starting point allows us to formulate definitions of the "good," the first of which is "what all desire."[6] Further consideration reveals that this is an imperfect definition: "what all desire" is a property of the good, but is not what makes the good, good. Things are not good because they are desired; they are desired because they are good. And so Aquinas reasons to a more perfect definition of good, namely, "what is perfective in the mode of a final cause":

> For the good is in things, as the Philosopher says in *Metaphysics*, Bk. VI . However, insofar as one being according to its being is perfective of another and completes it, it has the notion of an end with respect to that by which it is perfected; and whence it is that all rightly defining the good put in its notion something that pertains to the relationship of end; whence the Philosopher says in the *Ethics,* Bk. I, that those saying that the good is what all desire define the good most rightly. Thus, therefore, first and principally being perfective of another through the mode of an end is called good; but secondarily some is called good because it leads to the end, as the useful is called good....[7]

For example, health is good insofar as it is sought as a perfection of the living body, and food and exercise are goods insofar as they lead to this end; virtue is good insofar as it is sought as the perfection of the human soul, and discipline provided by parents is good insofar as it is a means to this end. In light of our understanding of what the good is, we are able to recognize that all non-rational beings are good: "Every being, insofar as it is a being, is in act and is in a certain manner perfect, for every act is a certain perfection. The perfect has the notion of desirable and good... Whence it follows that every being, insofar as it is such, is good."[8] We can thus recognize that non-rational natural things have inherent goodness. If these beings did not have a certain perfection, they would not be; all beings seek, though not necessarily consciously, to continue in existence as an end, and therein lies their good.[9] Thus, while we can see that non-rational beings are useful goods insofar as they are naturally meant to serve us, we can also see that in addition to this they have their own inherent perfection and goodness.

We know that the good ought to be loved; indeed nothing hates the good as such, but because it implies some contrariety to its appetite. One might object that what is good for fish is not good for humans; what perfects in each case is different,[10] and so humans have no reason to be concerned about things that are not good for them. Moreover, some natural things, such as mosquitoes, are harmful to humans, and we seek to eradicate them. Thus, Aquinas says:

> It manifestly appears in the case of natural appetite that every being whatsoever has a natural consonance or aptitude for what is suitable to it, which is what natural love is; so too, it has natural dissonance to that which is repugnant to it and corruptive of it, which is natural hatred. Therefore, in this manner in the animal appetite or the intellectual appetite, love is a certain consonance of the appetite to what it apprehends as suitable, [and] hatred is a certain dissonance of the appetite to what it apprehends as repugnant and harmful. However, just as every suitable thing, insofar as it is such, has the notion of the good; so also every repugnant thing, insofar as it is such, has the notion of bad. And therefore, just as the good is the object of love, so the bad is the object of hate.[11]

So human beings should hate mosquitoes. Granting this, we nonetheless should love all beings that are not harmful to us because we recognize them to be good as beings:

> Being, insofar as it is being, does not have the notion of what is repugnant, but rather of what is suitable, as all things agree in being. But being insofar as it is this determinate being has the notion of being repugnant to a certain determinate being. And according to this, one being is hateful to another and is bad, though not in itself, but in relation to the other.[12]

Likeness is a cause of love,[13] and therefore we should love all beings, insofar as they, like us, are beings. And this is true even in the case of mosquitoes and other beings harmful to us, though of course we do not love them insofar as they are harmful. For it is possible to love something from one point of view and hate it from another, e.g., we can love the medicine we take insofar as it will help restore us to health, but we can hate it insofar as it has a bad taste or disagreeable side-effects.[14] Aquinas thus defends the

goodness of all material creatures in the face of the Manichean argument that they sometimes harm us:
> The first error is that of the Manicheans who said that all visible things were created by the Devil…and the cause of this error is that not knowing how to discern what is bad and what is good, they believed that all things which were in some way bad, were simply speaking bad; as fire, because it burns, was said by them to be simply speaking bad, and water, because it drowns, and so forth.[15]

If we ought to love non-rational beings that are not harmful to us, and even those that are harmful to us to the extent that they are beings, a question still remains as to what sort of love we ought to extend to them. Aquinas takes up this question, relying on a distinction concerning love that was first articulated by Aristotle:
> Love is twofold…. Imperfect love of a thing is when someone loves something not so that he wishes the good for it for its sake, but he wishes the good of it for himself; and this manner of love is named by some "concupiscence," as when we love wine, we want to enjoy its sweetness, or when we love someone for the sake of our utility or pleasure. Another love, however, is perfect, by which we love the good of another for his own sake, as when loving someone, I want him to possess the good, even if nothing accrues to me from this; and for this reason it is called "love of friendship," by which someone is loved for his own sake.[16]

Aquinas applies this distinction to the case of non-rational creatures as follows; note that although he is speaking here about the supernatural virtue of charity, two of the reasons he gives hold true of love at the natural level:
> However, through friendship, the friend to whom friendship is had is loved in one manner, and the good which one wishes for the friend in another manner. Therefore, no non-rational creature is able to be loved out of charity in the first manner; and this for three reasons, two of which belong commonly to friendship, which cannot be had with non-rational creatures. [The other reason belongs properly to charity.] First,

because friendship is had towards him for whom we want the good. We are not, however, able to properly want the good to a non-rational creature because it does not properly possess the good, but only the rational creature does, who is a master using the good which he has through free will. And therefore the philosopher says, in Bk. II of the *Physics* that we do not say that something happens well or badly for such things, except by way of likeness. Secondly, because all friendship is founded upon some sharing of life, for there is nothing so proper to friendship as to share life together.... However, non-rational creatures are not able to have a share in human life which is according to reason. Whence no friendship can be had with non-rational creatures, except perhaps by way of metaphor.[17]

Certainly in some way plants and non-rational animals are able to possess goods, e.g., sufficient light and nutriments in the case of a plant, and food, shelter, etc. in the case of animals. However, they do not fully possess them because they are unaware that they are goods, as they have no concept of the good as such. This is clear in the case of non-conscious beings, such as plants. Even animals, however, are unable to assess the goodness of the particular goods they pursue. Sharks, for example, consciously seek to catch fish to eat. However, they do not have a conceptual understanding of the tie between the fish they eat and their health, much less any notion that they should consume fish in moderation or that they should consider befriending the fish, instead of eating them. The second reason Aquinas gives for why we are not to show non-rational creatures love of friendship is plain enough; they are incapable of being our friends, since they cannot share our life, insofar as we are capable of self-direction in virtue of possessing reason. Aquinas thus concludes: "Non-rational creatures are, nevertheless, able to be loved out of charity as goods which we want for others, insofar as namely from charity we want them to be preserved to the honor of God and the utility of men." It seems, then, that if it were not for God's honor being at stake, Aquinas would hold that non-rational natural things are only to be loved insofar as they are useful to us.

I think this view is somewhat over-simplified, and that Aquinas would agree with me here, as our love of non-rational creatures does not neatly fit into the categories of love of friendship and love of concupiscence, insofar as again we recognize that these beings have goodness apart from human utility. They are not pure instruments. A pure instrument has no goodness apart from its ability to serve a purpose. Once another instrument which better serves the purpose is discovered, it becomes obsolete and in effect "junk" (think of 8-track tapes or VCR tapes). Non-rational creatures, however, do have inherent goodness, and thus it is not entirely right for us to love them solely insofar as they serve us. Aquinas himself says as much in one passage where he speaks of God's love of non-rational creatures:

> It is required for genuine love (*ad veritatem amoris*) that one wants the good of another according as it is that other's good. For someone whose good one wants only insofar as it yields to the good of another is loved *per accidens*, just as he who wants to safeguard wine to drink it or a man to be useful or pleasurable to himself, loves that wine or man *per accidens*; per se he loves himself. But God wants the good of each and every thing according as it is its good; for he wants each thing to exist according as it is good in itself, granted he also orders one thing to the utility of another. Therefore, God truly loves both himself and other things.[18]

No creature is loved by God *solely* as an instrument. This does not mean, however, that non-rational creatures are not ordered by God to the utility of others, and that they are not primarily meant to serve others, namely, ourselves.

Accordingly, since we are both capable of understanding the inherent goodness of non-rational beings and of recognizing that they are inferior to us and are rightly used by us, we can see both that they ought not to be needlessly destroyed and that they may be destroyed to sustain our lives or when they pose a threat to human life. Thus, eradicating members of non-rational species is generally wrong; however, it is legitimate when the species poses a threat to human life (as for example is the case of mosquitoes that are vectors for deadly diseases).

NATURAL LAW DICTATES THAT HUMANS CARE FOR NON-RATIONAL NATURAL THINGS INSOFAR AS THE LATTER CONTRIBUTE TO THE GOOD OF THE COSMOS AND ULTIMATELY TO THE GLORY OF GOD

A second non-human centered argument for why we ought to care for the non-rational beings that make up the environment lies in our spontaneous recognition that non-rational beings are part of a greater whole, an ordered whole, a cosmos: "What is best, however, in created things is the perfection of the universe which consists in the order of distinct things. For in all things, the perfection of the whole surpasses the perfection of the individual parts."[19] This spontaneous recognition that we, along with other natural beings, are parts of a greater whole is witnessed to in many ways. For example, the psalmist writes: "I look at the moon and stars you set in place—ah, what is man that you should spare a thought for him, the son of man that you should care for him?" (Ps. 8:3-4) Eco-theologian Thomas Berry maintains that the attitude that we are parts of a greater whole is natural to pre-industrial societies. For example, he notes that:

> This continuity between the human and the cosmic was experienced also in the Chinese world, where the residence of the emperor was so arranged as to conform to the cardinal directions of the universe. Human activities through the year were coordinated with the cycle of the seasons. The clothes worn by member of the court, the music, the colors, the rituals were all carefully coordinated with the seasonal sequence. If summer music was played in the winter, then the entire cosmic order was considered to be disrupted. The supreme achievement of the human personality in this context was to experience one's own being as one body with heaven and Earth and the myriad things.[20]

The universe is not perceived as a mere collection of tools at our disposal. Accordingly, we should both love the greater goodness of the universe and of the individual species insofar as they contribute to it. Species contribute to the good of the universe insofar as they form part of a hierarchical chain of being[21] and insofar as their interaction with one another unifies the whole.[22]

The question arises then as to the sort of love with which we ought to love species insofar as they contribute to the goodness of the universe as a whole. A further question concerns how this love is to be balanced with the love we are to have for ourselves and our fellow humans. It might seem that we are called to sacrifice ourselves for the greater good of the order of the universe. Aquinas insists in many places:

> We see, however, that any part whatsoever by a certain natural inclination works for the good of the whole, even when this endangers it or is to its own detriment: as is manifest when someone exposes his hand to a sword for the defense of his head, on which the whole well-being of the body depends. Whence, it is natural that any part whatsoever loves the whole more than itself. Whence also according to this natural inclination, and according to political virtue, the good citizen exposes himself to the danger of death for the common good.[23]

It is not a question here of whether we should sacrifice ourselves for individual lower beings insofar as they are individuals, but whether we should do so insofar as they compose species whose hierarchy and interaction contribute to the greater good of the universe.[24] Perhaps it is not right, after all, to eradicate the mosquito or other species harmful to us. Do we have an obligation, as some people claim, to restrict how many children people have in order to protect species from extinction and unique ecosystems from destruction? Aquinas addresses this question, albeit in a theological context. First he raises an objection:

> God is loved with the love of charity. Therefore, what is principally loved by him ought to be more loved with the love of charity. But among all created things, what is principally loved by God is the good of the universe in which all things are comprehended. Therefore, all things are to be loved with the love of charity.[25]

Aquinas then responds:

> In the good of the universe, as what is principal, is the rational nature contained therein, which nature has the capacity for beatitude, [and] to which all other creatures are ordered; and according to this it belongs to God and to us to love with charity in the highest degree the good of the universe.[26]

Aquinas maintains that God loves the universe above all things because it is a whole whose parts are ordered to a being that can in some way share in the divine nature and enjoy friendship with God. Can a similar argument be mounted from a purely philosophical perspective, one that does not make reference to the Beatific Vision? I think it can be, though some parts of the argument are hotly debated. The argumentation here overlaps with that for what I propose is a third reason for caring for non-rational creatures. We will have to assume here that the argument(s) of Aristotle and/or Aquinas for the existence of God are cogent.

The question we need to consider is what is the end or purpose of the universe? Aquinas examines Aristotle's treatment of this question. He begins by noting:

> The Philosopher asks whether the nature of the whole universe has as what is good and best, that is, as its proper end, something as separated from it or does it have what is good and best in the order of its parts, in the manner in which the good of some natural thing is its form.[27]

Aquinas then comments on what he understands to be Aristotle's response:

> Therefore, he first says that the universe has its end and good in both ways. For there is some separate good which is the first mover from which the heavens and the whole of nature depends, as from an end and desirable good, as was shown.[28] And, because all things of whose end is one must agree in an order to the end, it is necessary that some order is found in the parts of the universe; and in this way, the universe has a separated good and the good of order; just as we see in an army. For the good of the army is both in the order of the army itself and in the leader who presides over

the army; but the good of the army is more in the leader than in the order, for the end is more potent in goodness than the things which are for the sake of an end. The order, however, of the army is for the sake of fulfilling the good of the leader, namely, the will of the leader in achieving victory; it is not however, vice versa, i.e., the good of the leader is not for the sake of the order. And, because the reason of things which are for the sake of an end are taken from the end, therefore it is necessary that not only the order of the army is for the sake of the leader, but also that the order of the army be from the leader, since the order of the army is for the sake of the leader. So also the separated good which is the first mover, is a better good than the good of order which is in the universe. For the whole order of the universe is for the sake of the first mover, so that, namely, what is in the intellect and will of the first mover is unfolded in the universe in an orderly manner. And thus it is necessary that the whole arrangement of the universe be from the first mover.[29]

It is commonly objected that Aristotle has been talking about God as a final cause and so interpreting the leader of an army as an efficient cause of the order of the universe is out-of-bounds. According to this view, God is closed within himself, and does not interact as an agent with other beings. However, Aristotle, at the end of the *Physics*, plainly concludes to the existence of God as prime mover in the sense of an efficient cause. And since God is the supreme good, he cannot act for an end other than himself. Thus, in moving things, he must move them to his own end. In the words of Aquinas:

> If many agents have an order, it is necessary that the actions and motions of every agent are ordered to the good of the first agent, as to an ultimate end. For since the lower agents are moved by the higher agent, and every mover moves to his own end, it is necessary that the actions and motions of the lower agents tend to the end of the higher agent: just as in an army, the actions of all orders are ordered to victory as ultimate, which is the end of the leader. It has been shown above, however, that the first mover and agent is God.[30]

Elsewhere Aquinas explains how we are to understand God himself to be the end of his moving (and presumably creating[31]) other beings:

> In order to understand in what manner God makes and wants all things for the sake of his goodness one must know that that something is done for the sake of an end can be understood in two ways: either for the sake of an end to be attained, as a sick person takes medicine for the sake of health, or for the sake of the love of an end to be spread, as a doctor operates for the sake of health that is to be communicated to another. God, however, is in need of no good exterior to himself.... And therefore when it is said that God wants and makes all things for the sake of his goodness, it is not to be understood that he makes something for the sake of imparting goodness to himself, but for the sake of spreading it to others.[32]

God has himself as ultimate end in imparting goodness to others, insofar as these beings give him glory. God is not in need of this glory,[33] but it is nonetheless directed to him.[34] He is the most perfect of agents and so "it belongs to him to introduce his likeness in created things in the most perfect manner as suits created nature."[35] A masterpiece manifests the skill of the artist, and thus gives him glory. Accordingly, "the whole universe, with its individual parts, is ordered to God as to an end, insofar as in them a certain imitation of divine goodness is represented to the glory of God."[36]

Non-rational creatures give glory to God by their individual inherent goodness[37] and above all by their ordering to the greater whole that is the universe.[38] Rational creatures are able to give glory to God in the full sense of glory because they can knowingly and lovingly praise God for his goodness. Thus, Aquinas continues the passage above with the affirmation:

> However, divine goodness is imparted to the rational creature, properly speaking, so that the rational creature itself knows it. And thus everything which God makes in the case of rational creatures, he creates to his praise and glory,

according to Is. 43:7: 'Everyone who calls on my name, I have created him for my glory,' namely, that he might know [God's] goodness and knowing it praise it.[39]

The rest of the material universe would be imperfectly ordered to God's glory if rational beings such as ourselves were absent in it, since we alone, upon contemplating the order of creation, can go on to consciously give glory to God.[40]

We find then reasons for us to care for species and the ecosystems in which they interact from philosophical arguments that show that this order comes from God and is meant to give him glory. To needlessly disrupt or destroy the order of nature is thus contrary to the reverence that we ought to show God. This does not mean, however, that we cannot destroy a species if doing so is necessary for saving human lives, because it is primarily through us that the end of the universe is achieved; only rational beings can in the full sense give glory to God, and this is true of each and every human individual.[41]

DOES NATURAL LAW DICTATE THAT HUMANS CARE FOR NON-RATIONAL NATURAL THINGS INSOFAR AS THE LATTER CONTRIBUTE TO THE GOOD OF THE UNIVERSE INDEPENDENTLY OF THE UNIVERSE'S ORDERING TO GOD?

Can the second argument I've proposed above stand without bringing in God's glory as the ultimate goal of the universe, i.e., does the notion that species contribute to the universe as a whole, which is a greater good of which we are only a part, of itself provide a compelling reason for us to be morally obligated to avoid destroying them?

It would be misguided to think that one could judge how we should interact with other parts of a whole to which we belong while ignoring the further end to which that whole is ordered; again, "the order, however, of the army is for the sake of fulfilling the good of the leader."[42] We also must not forget that the nobler naturally uses the less noble, and this ordering comes from God. Non-rational beings are capable of simultaneously contributing to the good of the universe, serving humans, and giving glory to God, and we are capable of treating them in ways that respect all of these ends. As Aquinas explains in response to an objector who maintains that the ordering of lower things to higher things runs counter to the ordering of lower things to the universe as a whole:

> [A]ll of the parts are thus ordered to the perfection of the whole insofar as one serves another. As in the human body, it is apparent that the lungs belong to the perfection of the body because they serve the heart: whence it is not contrary for the lungs to be for the sake of the heart, and for the sake of the whole animal. And similarly it is not contrary for other natures to exist for the sake of intellectual beings and for the sake of the perfection of the universe: for if those things which the perfection of the intellectual substance require were lacking, the universe would not be complete.[43]

It would be a mistake to deny that we as parts of the universe have a natural inclination to preserve its good, one that is other than the natural inclination that we have in virtue of our specifically rational nature to revere God. There is plenty of evidence that this is the case. As noted earlier, many non-technological peoples have customs based on their perception of themselves as part of a greater whole and regard actions contrary to these customs as morally wrong. Members of certain tribes of American Indians felt a need to apologize to the animals they killed as they regarded them as fellow inhabitants of this world, as kin in a circle of nature.[44] This tendency is also witnessed to by its excess in the various forms of nature worship and in the views of those environmentalists who maintain that human beings are a cancer on the earth because our increasing population results in habitat destruction and extinction, along with those who maintain that we ought to insure species preservation even at the cost of human lives. However, this natural tendency, one which we share along with all other substances, has to be followed in keeping with our rational nature, just as the natural inclinations to preserve ourselves, and thus to consume food and drink, are not to be blindly followed, but need to be perfected by the virtue of temperance whose mean is determined by reason.

Thus, while the natural inclination of a part to preserve the whole indicates as a dictate of natural law that we avoid needless destruction of species and ecosystems which would damage the integrity of the whole, at the same time, our privileged position in realizing the end to which the universe is ordered, namely God's glory, measures the extent to which this inclination is to be followed. Thus, it would be contrary to reason and to virtue to follow the inclination to preserve species and ecosystems when it would entail the loss of a human life.[45]

OBSTACLES TO THE NATURAL LAW APPROACH TO ENVIRONMENTALISM

We have seen, then, that the natural law approach proposes three non-human-centered reasons for caring for the environment: two based on natural inclinations we have in virtue of our nature as rational beings, and one based on a natural inclination we share with all substances. There are a number of obstacles to accepting this approach. The first set of obstacles concerns knowledge about God and the reverence we owe God. Some environmentalists reject God's existence and some hold pantheistic notions of God. The natural law position depends on knowledge of God as separate from creation and as ordering all creation to himself; and as ordering the rational creature to himself in a very special way. Without this knowledge, the notion that we as parts should sacrifice ourselves for the good of the whole would seem to be unqualifiedly true. As for the reverence we owe God, it must be said that although it "belongs to a dictate of natural law that man does certain things to reverence God,"[46] without supernatural faith, human beings generally have a very imperfect knowledge of this dictate; even Aristotle, who does mention the virtue of religion on a number of occasions, neither discusses it at any length nor names it as the highest moral virtue.

Another reason why people are apt to reject a natural law approach is because they reject the notion that humans are superior to other natural beings. It is not uncommon for environmentalists to claim that any and every species is equal in value to the human species and that our species has no more right to be on the planet than other species do. At the root of this problem is the failure to understand what reason is and to see that humans are the only earthly beings that possess it. I have not undertaken in this paper to distinguish reason from the internal sense powers often mistaken for it, nor have I defended the notion that the possession of reason is part of what defines humans as human. A treatment of these points is essential to a full understanding of the natural law arguments that I have given.[47]

Yet another obstacle to the natural law approach is that it relies on concepts that are unfamiliar to many environmentalists (e.g., the division of love into love of friendship and love of concupiscence) or that appear to them as abstract and distant from the concrete realities of pollution, habitat loss, etc., that they are trying to address (e.g., the concepts of the good and of the relationship between final and efficient causality).

Something that can pose an obstacle to those familiar with the Aristotelian-Thomistic tradition are Aquinas's repeated affirmations that non-rational creatures are not to be loved with the love of friendship. This can lead one to too quickly conclude that our love of non-rational beings should be solely that of love of concupiscence in its strictest sense. As I have argued above, the dichotomy between love of friendship and love of concupiscence does not neatly capture the love we should have for non-rational substances, for granted they cannot be rightly loved by us in the manner in which we love those who share the life of reason with us, nonetheless, they have their own inherent goodness which makes them loveable independent of their utility to us.

CONCLUSION

While natural law reasoning leads to the notion that it is right for us to make use of non-rational creatures to sustain our lives and promote our well-being, it does not support the notion that they are to be cared for merely as tools for our use. Rather, it also entails three non-human-centered directives as to their care. Two of the latter derive from the natural inclination which is proper to human beings as human, i.e., to know the truth (above all the highest truths, i.e., about God, but other truths as well). A truth that reason can apprehend is that non-rational creatures have inherent goodness. In addition, reason can grasp the kind of the love that ought to be shown them insofar as they, like ourselves, are beings: a love that, while falling short of the love of friendship, due to their inability to share in the life of reason, corresponds to the goodness these things possess apart from our use of them. A second dictate stems from reason's ability to recognize God as both orderer and ultimate end of the universe. Since God orders non-rational creatures to his glory, and not merely to human usage, to needlessly destroy the universe's divinely established order, which consists in diverse species and their interactions, is contrary to the reverence that we ought to show God. A third dictate of natural law is rooted in an inclination we share with other substances, namely, the inclination of a part to protect the good of the whole to which it belongs. Reason recognizes, however, that the dictate to safeguard non-rational species in order to preserve the integrity of the whole must be followed in keeping with the special place that humans have in that whole insofar as it is further ordered to God. For only rational beings are capable of giving glory to God in the full sense of the word and are capable of sharing in God's happiness.

NOTES

1. In speaking about natural law I am referring to Aquinas's understanding of it as found in *Summa Theologiae*, I-II, 94.2: "All those things to be done or avoided which practical reason naturally apprehends to be human goods may pertain to precepts of nature law. Because the good has the notion of an end, and bad the contrary notion, whence it is that all those things to which man has a natural inclination, reason naturally apprehends as good, and consequently to be pursued in deed, and the contraries of them as bad and to be avoided. Therefore, according to the order of natural inclination is the order of precepts of natural law. For in man there is first an inclination to the good which he share with all substances, according as each and every substance

desires to preserves its being according to its nature. And according to this inclination, those things by which the life of man is preserved and the contrary impeded pertain to natural law. ... In a third manner, there is an inclination in man to the good according to the nature of reason, which is proper to him, as man has a natural inclination to this that he knows the truth about God and to this that he lives in society. Accordingly, those things which regard the inclination of this sort pertain to natural law, such as that man avoid ignorance, that he not offend others with whom he ought to have social intercourse, and other such things that regard it." Hereafter cited as *ST*. Unless otherwise noted, all texts from Aquinas are drawn from the online *Corpus Thomisticum*, ed. Enrique Alarcón, University of Navarre, http://www.corpusthomisticum.org/iopera.html. All translations are my own.
2. See Aristotle, *Politics*, Bk. 1, c. 8, 1256b7-26.
3. *ST* II-II, q. 66, a. 1. See also, *ST* I, q. 96 a. 1: "However, all animals are naturally subject to man; which appears from three things: first, from very course of nature. For just as a certain order is understood in the generation of things by which it proceeds from imperfect to perfect (for matter is for the sake of form, and the more imperfect forms for the more perfect ones), so too in the use of natural things, for the less perfect yield to the use of the perfect; for plants use the earth for their nutrition, animals use plants, and man uses plants and animals. Whence, man naturally rules the animals. And for this reason the philosopher says in Bk. 1 of the *Politics*, that hunting wild animals is just and natural because through it man claims for himself what is naturally his."
4. See *ST* II-II, q. 66, a. 7: "According to the natural order instituted by divine providence, lower things are ordered to the end that human necessity be alleviated from them. And therefore the division and appropriation of things proceeding from human law may not impede that human need be alleviated by things of this sort."
5. *Summa contra Gentiles*, Bk. II, chap. 23. (Hereafter cited as *SCG*.)
6. *ST* I, q. 5, a. 4 and ad 1.
7. *De veritate*, q. 21 a. 1.
8. *ST* I, q. 5, a .3.
9. See *SCG*, Bk. III, chap. 19: "In all things it is evidently apparent that they naturally desire to be; whence if they are able to be corrupted by something, they naturally resist what can corrupt them, and they tend to that place where they are preserved, as fire upwards and earth downwards." I acknowledge that this is not obviously true in the case of non-living natural things; however, it is plainly true in the case of living things.
10. *ST* I-II, q. 27, a. 1: "The proper object of love is the good, for...love implies a certain connaturality or agreeability of the lover to the beloved; the good for each, however, is what is connatural or proportioned to it."
11. *ST* I-II, q. 29, a. 1.

12. *ST* I-II, q. 29, a. 1, ad 1.
13. See *ST* I-II, q. 27, a. 3.
14. See *ST* I, q. 20, a. 2, ad 4: "Nothing prevents one and the same thing to be loved according to something and to be held in hatred according to something. God loves sinners insofar as they are of a certain nature; for in this manner they both are and are from him. Insofar as they are sinners, however, they are not, but draw away from being, and this in them is not from God. Whence according to this, they are held in hatred by him."
15. In *Symbolum Apostolorum*, a. 1.
16. *De Spe*, unicus, a. 3.
17. *ST* II-II, q. 25, a. 3.
18. *SCG* I, chap. 91. See also, *De Veritate*, q. 27, a. 1: "For God to accept or love something, which is the same thing, is nothing other than to want some good for it. For God wants for every creature the good of nature, on account of which all things are said to be loved: 'You love all the things that are, and you approve of all of them' (Ws. 11:25); 'God saw all that he made [and indeed it was very good]' (Gn. 1:31)."
19. *SCG* II, chap. 45.
20. Thomas Berry, *Evening Thoughts: Reflecting on Earth as Sacred Community* (Sierra Club Books, 2006), 50. See also, ibid., 110: "They [earlier peoples] lived in a pattern of human activities that were validated by their relation with the cosmological sequence. They lived with the Covenant of the Universe, the ontological covenant whereby each component of the universe experienced itself in intimate rapport with the other components of the universe."
21. See *Commentary on De Anima*, lib. 2, l. 5: "To this that the universe be perfect no grade of perfection is omitted in things, but nature little by little proceeds from the imperfect to the perfect. On account of which Aristotle also assimilates the species of things to numbers which progress little by little." See also *De ente et essentia*, chap. 4: "But diverse grades of perfections in the forms and natures shared [by individuals] diversifies species, as nature proceeds through grades from plants to animals through certain things which are intermediary between animals and plants," according to the Philosopher in Bk. VII of *De Animalibus*.
22. See *ST* I, q. 103, a. 4, ad 1: "The order of the universe includes in itself both the conservation of the diverse things instituted by God, and the motion of them; because according to these a twofold order is found in things, namely, according as one thing is better than another, and according as one thing is moved by another."
23. *Quodlibet* I, q. 4, a. 3. See also, *De Spe*, a. 1, ad 9 and *ST* II-II, q. 26, a. 3.
24. See *ST* I, q. 70, a. 2, ad 4: "Nevertheless, nothing prohibits that it be said that the more worthy creature is made for the lower creature, not according as the latter is considered in itself, but according as it is ordered to the integrity of the universe."
25. *Quaestio Disputata de caritate*, unicus, a. 7, obj. 5.

26. Ibid., ad 5.
27. *Commentary on the Metaphysics*, Bk. XII, lec. 12 (no. 2628 in the Marietti edition).
28. See Aristotle, *Metaphysics*, in *The Basic Works of Aristotle*, ed. Richard McKeon (New York: Random House, 1968), 1072a23: "Therefore the first heaven must be eternal. There is therefore also something which moves it. And since that which is moved and moves is intermediate, there is something which moves without being moved, being eternal, substance and actuality. And the object of desire and thought move in this way; they move without being moved." Given that there is reason to question whether motion in the universe has been eternal, there is reason to question Aristotle's conclusion that there is an eternal, unmoved, end of the universe. However, if the universe came to be at some time, this arguably requires an eternal and unchanging final cause.
29. *Commentary on the Metaphysics*, Bk. XII, lec. 12.
30. *Compendium Theologiae*, chap. 103.
31. I think a case can be made that God not only moves things in the universe to his end, but he also creates things for the sake of his goodness; I cannot pursue this matter here, but refer the reader to Mark Johnson's article "Did St. Thomas Attribute a Doctrine of Creation to Aristotle," *New Scholasticism*, 63, 2 (1989), 129-155.
32. *Commentary on Ephesians* in *Super Epistolas S. Pauli*, ed. P. Raphaelis Cai, O.P., vol. 2, (Rome: Marietti, 1953), #13. See also *ST* I, q. 19, a. 2 and *Quaestiones Disputatae de Potentia* q. 3, a. 15, ad 14.
33. See *SCG* III, chap. 18: "God, however, who is the first agent of all things, does not act in such as manner as if he were to acquire something from his action, but in such a manner that he bestows something by his action: for he is not in potency such that he could be able to acquire something, but he is only in perfect act, from which he is able to bestow something." See also *ST* II-II, q. 81, a. 7.
34. See *SCG* III, chap. 17: "There is no other end of his [God's] will than his goodness which is himself."
35. *SCG* II, 45.
36. Ibid.
37. The goodness inherent in the things themselves does not preclude their ordering to God's goodness, but rather is what allows them to be ordered to it; see *ST* I, q. 47, a. 1: "God produces things for the sake of communicating his goodness to creatures, and through them to represent his goodness."
38. See *ST* I 47. 1: "God produces things for the sake of communicating his goodness to creatures, and through them to represent his goodness. And because it cannot be adequately represented through one creature, he produces many and diverse creatures, so that what is lacking in one for the purpose of representing divine goodness, is filled up by others; for the goodness which exists simply and uniformly in God, in creatures is multiple and divided.

Whence the whole universe more perfectly shares in and represents divine goodness than any other creature whatsoever."

39. *Commentary on Ephesians* #13. See also, *ST* I, q. 65, a. 2: "Further, moreover, the whole universe, with its individual parts, are ordered to God as to an end, insofar as divine goodness is represented in them by means of a certain imitation, to the glory of God; although rational creatures have God as their end in a certain special mode beyond this, whom they can attain by their own operation, by knowing and loving [him]. And thus it is manifest that divine goodness is the end of all corporeal beings."

40. See *Quaestio Disputata de Spiritualibus Creaturis*, unicus, 6, obj. 14: "To praise, to relate, and to exult do not belong to anything but the living and knowing thing. But...according to the psalm...the heavens proclaim the glory of God." Aquinas responds: "According to Damascene, the heavens are said to proclaim the glory of God, to praise [him], to exult [him], in a material manner, insofar as they are matter for men to praise or proclaim or exult [God]. Similar things are found in Scripture concerning mountains and hills and other inanimate creatures." See also, *Disputed Question on the Soul*, a. 8, ad 19.

41. See *SCG* III, chap. 112: "Moreover, whenever there are things that are ordered to some end, if some among them of themselves are not able to attain the end, it is necessary that they be ordered to the things which do attain the end, [i.e.,] to the things which for their own sake are ordered to the end; as the end of the army is victory which soldiers attain through their own act of fighting, who alone are wanted for their own sakes in the army. All others, however, are charged with other duties, e.g., taking care of horses, preparing arms, [etc.] for the sake of the soldiers who are wanted in the army. From what has been said earlier, it stands that God is the ultimate end of the universe, which only the intellectual nature can attain in itself, namely, by knowing and loving him.... Therefore, only the intellectual nature is prized (quaesita) in the universe, and other things for its sake."

42. *Commentary on the Metaphysics*, Bk. XII, lec. 12. See also, *ST* I-II, q. 109, a. 3: "It is manifest, however, that the good of the part is for the sake of the good of the whole. Whence, also, by natural appetite and love each and every particular thing loves its own good for the sake of the common good of the universe, which is God."

43. *SCG* III, chap. 112.

44. Christopher Vecsey and Robert W. Venables, eds., *American Indian Environments: Ecological Issues in Native American History* (Syracuse, NY: Syracuse University Press, 1994), 23.

45. Paintings generally need to be framed, and the framed painting is more beautiful than the unframed one. It would make no sense, though, for the painting to sacrifice itself for the frame. Similarly, the universe is more perfect than the rational beings which are part of it, but it would make no sense for the

latter to sacrifice themselves for another part of the whole in order to protect the integrity of the whole.
46. *ST* II-II, q. 81, a. 2.
47. In regard to how humans excel other animals, see: "Thomas Aquinas Meets Nim Chimpsky: On the Debate About Human Nature and the Nature of Other Animals," *The Aquinas Review*, 10, 2003, 1-50.

THE RATIONAL ORDER OF NATURE AND THE ENVIRONMENTAL IMPLICATIONS OF NATURAL LAW

James M. Jacobs

INTRODUCTION

Pope Francis's encyclical *Laudato Si'* has been described as an "environmental encyclical." This radically undervalues its point, for throughout Francis identifies environmental problems with a more fundamental crisis: the erosion of man's sense of a moral order which affects human society *first*. The primary environment for man, as a spiritual being, is always the *moral* environment; other environmental issues are symptomatic of man's relation to this moral order. Accordingly, Francis begins by acknowledging his predecessor and arguing, "Pope Benedict asked us to recognize that the natural environment has been gravely damaged by our irresponsible behavior. The social environment has also suffered damage. Both are ultimately due to the same evil: the notion that there are no indisputable truths to guide our lives, and hence human freedom is limitless."[1] Francis is clearly tracing the crises of environment and society to modernity's rejection of objective truth,[2] which ineluctably vitiates man's relation both to other people and to the world at large. This rejection of objective order is the fruit of a metaphysical nominalism,[3] in which a teleological ordering of natures to the good is replaced by a merely mechanistic universe which is to be manipulated by technological virtuosity in satisfaction of human desire.[4] Thus, for Francis, the ultimate problem is man's rejection of a real metaphysical order which not only informs the human good in terms of the natural law, but also which disposes nature as a whole to be ordered toward an inherent perfection of its own. Indeed, the two are necessarily intertwined, for the natural law orders man to perfection in terms of intellectual understanding, but that understanding is then called on to know and respect the order of nature.[5] Indeed, wisdom itself—putting all things in their right place—is nothing other than a respect for the Creator's ordering of nature.[6]

Therefore, in order to address these social and environmental crises, it is necessary to recover the wisdom that unites the natural moral law and the laws of nature.[7] This can be done by demonstrating that there is a rational order in nature as a *necessary* aspect of creation. In fact, the evidence for such a rational order is manifold. More commonly, arguments demonstrating this are made inductively from man's empirical experience of regularity in nature, which can only be explained by an Aristotelian realism in which real universal principles unite disparate beings into species.[8] However, I will argue that the necessity of a natural order can also be argued deductively according to the principles of the metaphysics of being (though the specific content of those laws are, of course, only known *a posteriori*). In this paper, I show how an intelligible order in nature is necessary because contingent being requires a principle of potentiality which determines that being (and its concomitant activity) according to a natural kind. Further, the convertibility of the transcendentals means that this order is knowable and must be respected. Finally, I will show how this argument underlies the vision of *Laudato Si'* inasmuch as the natural law necessarily implies a prudent stewardship of the environment according to the principles by which nature itself is ordered by God.

THE DEDUCTIVE METAPHYSICAL ARGUMENT FOR THE NECESSITY OF LAWS OF NATURE

A fundamental problem for those who would argue that creation entails a necessary natural order is the doctrine of divine omnipotence. If an order in creation is necessary, then God cannot really be omnipotent and free; on the other hand, if God is omnipotent and free, there need be nothing necessary in the cosmos as we experience it. However, if it can be shown that there is a necessary order even in spite of the doctrine of divine freedom, then it would be clear that this ordering of nature cannot be intelligently denied.

Thomas accomplishes this in his exposition of how Providence embodies a rational plan in *Summa Contra Gentiles* III.97.[9] As Thomas points out, this balanced position avoids two sorts of errors about God and creation: "There is the mistake of those who believe that all things follow, without any rational plan, from God's pure will. This is the error of the exponents of the Law of the Moors.... Also refuted is the error of those who say that the order of causes comes forth from divine providence by way of necessity."[10] Thus, against the first error, Thomas denies the voluntarist assertion that divine freedom implies there is no rational order in creation, as Islam (and Christian nominalists) hold;[11] on the other hand, against the second, Thomas asserts that these necessary reasons in creation do not limit God's freedom, as in Spinoza's monism. Thomas seeks to establish a middle position: God is utterly free in creating, but that whatever He chooses to create must necessarily embody certain rational principles which are manifested in the objective intelligibility of the laws of nature. This becomes the foundation uniting the laws of nature (teleological regularity of creatures) with the natural law (man's practically directive knowledge based on understanding that teleological regularity).

The argument in *SCG* III.97 has four steps: (1) God freely creates to manifest His goodness; (2) God's goodness necessitates a multiplicity of creatures; (3) a multiplicity of creatures is attained only by means of necessary ontological principles to diversify being; (4) the subsequent activity of creatures follows with necessity from those principles and so manifests law-like regularity. In sum, there are necessary reasons in God's providential plan, for He must diversify creatures by means of metaphysical principles, yet this in no way impugns His freedom in creating, for He could have created any creatures He wished.[12] Thus even an omnipotent God cannot create a world without intelligible objective order; nominalism's presumption is, then, utterly impossible. Consequently, it is incumbent on man to respect the natural order of creation, for to reject it can only result in disorder for both man and his environment.

I will now elucidate the argument from *SCG* III.97 to establish the metaphysical grounding of the environmental implications of natural law.

THE FREEDOM OF CREATION

The argument begins with an affirmation of God's transcendent freedom by reminding us of the utter contingency of creation: God is under no necessity to create, but simply wants to share His goodness with creatures: "God, through His providence, orders all things to the divine goodness, as to an end; not, of course, in such a way that something adds to His goodness by means of things that are made, but, rather, that the likeness of His goodness, as much as possible, is impressed on things."[13]

This desire to share His goodness is utterly gratuitous, for as a perfect being, God wills only Himself and has no need for creation: "God wills His own goodness necessarily, even as we will our own happiness necessarily.... But God wills things apart from Himself in so far as they are ordered to His own goodness as their end."[14] God is therefore completely free in willing creation. The only reason for creation is the sheer self-diffusiveness of the good:

> For natural things have a natural inclination not only towards their own proper good, to acquire it if not possessed, and, if possessed, to rest therein; but also to spread abroad their own good amongst others, so far as possible.... It pertains, therefore, to the nature of the will to communicate as far as possible to others the good possessed; and especially does this pertain to the divine will, from which all perfection is derived in some kind of likeness.[15]

The gratuitous nature of creation, in conjunction with God's infinite will, means that He could have created *anything*.[16] That He shares the goodness of being with those whom He chooses highlights the radical giftedness of nature[17] to which *Laudato Si'* calls our attention. Thus, God's freedom is radical and fundamental: He did not have to create at all, and in creating, His will is not limited or determined in any way.

However, in order to share His goodness in creation, we discover two metaphysical principles which will lead us to the necessity of an intelligible order of nature. Goodness implies, first, *existence* itself as the perfection of being; and second, the need for diversification of being according to intelligible principles. Thus, it is the principle of being itself which grounds creation's rational order.

God seeks to share His goodness, but *good* is defined as being under the aspect of desirability;[18] in particular, it is the perfection of existence that is desired as good.[19] Thus, to share goodness, God creates—gives existence to creatures *ex nihilo*. Only God, who is the subsistent act of existence,[20] can create,[21] and all things other than God must be created by Him: "All beings apart from God are not their own being, but are beings by participation. Therefore it must be that all things which are diversified by the diverse participation of being, so as to be more or less perfect, are caused by one First Being, Who possesses being most perfectly."[22] To put this another way, the fact that all created beings, regardless of their myriad differences, share the property of existence points to a higher cause whose nature it is to cause existence.[23]

Thus, in creation, being, as the most universal effect, is the proper effect of the primary agent of all things.[24] But, again, this means that God is utterly free to create anything, since He is bringing it out of nothing and so His activity has no pre-existing limitations.[25] This understanding of creation, by which the existence of all things is grounded in God's desire to share the goodness of His own existence, clearly answers the metaphysical puzzle of why there is anything at all. But a second metaphysical puzzle remains: If there is no necessity in creation, why does it display an intelligible order? Thomas's answer has already been suggested: there are *diverse participations in being*. These diverse participations mean that there are degrees of perfection which provide an order to creation.

The Necessity of a Plurality of Creatures

Thomas insists that to represent His infinite goodness, God has to create a multiplicity of finite beings:

Since every created substance must fall short of the perfection of divine goodness, in order that the likeness of divine goodness might be more perfectly communicated to things, it was necessary for there to be a diversity of things, so that what could not be perfectly represented by one thing might be, in more perfect fashion, represented by a variety of things in different ways.... [T]hat perfect goodness which is present in God in a unified and simple manner cannot be in creatures except in a diversified manner through the plurality of things.[26]

This, however, presents a problem: how can the simple and infinite act of existence in God be made diverse and finite? Being in itself is infinite and undifferentiated because it is, in Thomas's oft-quoted teaching, the "actuality of all acts, and therefore the perfection of all perfections"[27]; it is the universal cause of all that is, for it "is that which makes every form or nature actual."[28] In this sense, existence is identical in all beings: it is the same one creative act that flows from God to all creatures.[29]

The initial resolution lies in the notion that diverse participations in being are *possible* because of the multiplicity of the divine ideas.[30] The principle of divine simplicity means that God knows only Himself; yet, that single act of knowing generates a multiplicity of ideas because in knowing His own infinite act of existence, He knows all the various ways in which being can be participated:

> Inasmuch as God knows His own essence perfectly, He knows it according to every mode in which it can be known. Now it can be known not only as it is in itself, but as it can be participated in by creatures according to some degree of likeness. But every creature has its own proper species, according to which it participates in some degree in likeness to the divine essence.[31]

The divine essence, then, is *simultaneously* the source of common existence as well as the exemplar of created diversity. God wills things into being, but the diversity of those things follows from the divine intellect and so displays a rational order: "Now it is manifest that things made by nature receive determinate forms. This determination of forms must be reduced to the divine wisdom as its first principle, for divine wisdom devised the order of the universe, which order consists in the variety of things. And therefore we must say that in the divine wisdom are the types of all things."[32] Thus, in order to best represent His infinite goodness, God's ideas act as exemplars of diverse participations in existence.

The Principles by which Plurality is Achieved

Though the exemplars explain how diversity is possible, it can only be realized by means of an immanent formal cause modeled on the exemplar's mode of being which delimits the act of existence in concrete substances. Thomas, therefore, next takes up form as the cause of differentiation into species: "The reason for the order of things is derived from the diversity of forms. Indeed, since it is in accord with its form that a thing has being, and since anything, in so far as it has being, approaches the likeness of God Who is His own simple being, it must be that form is nothing else than a divine likeness that is participated in things."[33]

Forms can act as principles of diversification of being because this is an application of the fundamental Thomistic principle that act is diversified by a receptive potency; in receiving act, the receptive potency limits it to a specific mode. "Every act inhering in another is terminated by that in which it inheres, since what is in another is in it according to the mode of the receiver"; or, again, with respect to existence in particular, "Considered absolutely, being is infinite, since there are infinite and infinite modes in which it can be participated. If, then, the being of some thing is finite, that being must be limited by something other that is somehow its cause."[34] Therefore, in creation God gives the act of existence, but that act can only be limited by that which was in potency to existence, the form or essence of a finite creature.[35] Thus, no creature *qua* creature is being simply; every creature must be a *kind* of being. Created forms, then, are the principle of potency which delimits received being and diversifies it.[36]

But since difference between creatures is determined by the varying degrees of participation in existence, the result is a hierarchy of being:

> Now, the nearer a thing comes to divine likeness, the more perfect it is. Consequently, there cannot be a difference among forms unless because one thing exists more perfectly than another.... [T]he diversity of things is accomplished by means of gradations. Indeed, he will find plants above inanimate bodies, and above plants irrational animals, and above these intellectual substances.[37]

The created universe, then, is a plenum of diverse gradations of perfection which together manifest the infinite goodness of God.

It may be objected that this necessary diversity could just be a multitude of individuals and that there need not be universal kinds. Thomas, however, rejects this, because this would fail to embody the maximal good: "The good of the species is greater than the good of the individual, just as the formal exceed that which is material. Hence, a multiplicity of species adds more to the goodness of the universe than a multiplicity of individuals in one species."[38] Moreover, this multiplicity of species is not simply an amorphous variety, but is rather an ordered distinction in which creatures symbiotically provide for one another in that their activity is mutually ordered to the perfection of the universe, for "no creature could act for the benefit of another creature unless plurality and inequality existed in created things."[39] Therefore, for creation to represent God's goodness, it is clear that God must create different kinds of things to represent different grades of goodness; and this can be accomplished only by a diversity of forms to limit the act of existence.[40]

This multiplicity of creatures, however, does not entail only a variety of species, but also a variety of individuals within species. That is, to best represent God's goodness, some species are constituted so that many individuals express all the potential goodness of that mode of being. For example, no one person exhausts all the possible perfections of human nature; each individual has his own gifts. This, however, means that there must be *another* principle by which that specific form is individuated:

> A twofold distinction is found in things; one is a formal distinction as regards things differing specifically; the other is a material distinction as regards things differing numerically only. And as the matter is on account of the form, material distinction exists for the sake of the formal distinction.... Therefore...divine wisdom is the cause of the distinction of things for the sake of the perfection of the universe.[41]

Moreover, the instantiation of a form in matter is never haphazard or arbitrary; on the contrary, since matter exists for the sake of the form, it must be integrally proportioned to the form: "Now, matter and form could not combine to make up one thing unless there were some proportion between them. But, if they must be proportionally related, then different matters must correspond to different forms."[42] This unique combination of form and matter composes the essence of the substance[43] which receives the act of existence to constitute created being: "The form and the matter [must] be joined together in the unity of one act of being.... And this single act of being is that in which the composite substance subsists: a thing one in being and made up of matter and form."[44]

Thus, in every created being, there in an intelligible order of causal principles by which being is determined to a determinate mode: "In created things...there are diverse modes of necessity arising from diverse causes. For, since a thing cannot be without its essential principles which are matter and form, whatever belongs to a thing by reason it its essential principles must have absolute necessity in all cases."[45] The necessary intelligibility of this follows from the fact that the act of existence, which is the *sine qua non* of all contingent beings, must be limited by ontological principles in order to yield distinct species and individuals.[46]

The Providential Order of the Activity

The last step in Thomas's argument is that diverse natures act with a regularity such that we can know them according to the laws of nature:

Now, from the diversity of forms by which the species of things are differentiated there also results a difference of operations. For, since everything acts in so far as it is actual...and since every being is actual through form, it is necessary for the operation of a thing to follow its form. Therefore, if there are different forms, they must have different operations.[47]

Action follows from being: the act of existence, as *act*, imparts a dynamism to created substances; but that dynamism reflects the limitation of existence by the essence.[48] Indeed, the diversification of form is really for the sake of these diverse modes of acting: "For the less perfect is always for the sake of the more perfect: and consequently as the matter is for the sake of the form, so the form which is the first act, is for the sake of its operation, which is the second act."[49] In this way, the apparently chaotic diversity and dynamism of the universe are in fact reduced to providentially ordered intelligible principles. This diversity of action is necessary for a perfect universe, for each creature does what God deems necessary to attain the perfection of the whole. The laws of nature by which the substances act in a determinately regular fashion, then, are not simply mechanistic facts, but are the very activity by which God's goodness is realized in creation.

The work of nature, then, must be respected as of divine origin; while the causality of nature is immanent and mundane and knowable by science, that causal order necessarily implies a higher mode of causality which constitutes it in being. It is the rejection of this that is the very problem Francis decries in *Laudato Si'*. It is for this reason, too, that Thomas can say that secondary causes are the executors of divine providence[50] since, while "God acts perfectly as first cause...the operation of nature as second cause is also necessary...[for] He wishes to act by means of nature in order to preserve order in things."[51] God shares His goodness not just in making things exist, but by differentiating them and ordering them to diverse perfective activity.[52] Nor is this cooperation of creation with God repugnant to divine omnipotence, for omnipotence means to be able to do everything that is possible; yet it is a contradiction in terms to say that the act of existence can be limited without some principle of potency.[53] Thus, God necessarily employs intelligible ontological causes to limit being. It is clear, then, that all created beings are beings of definite kind, and their regular activity is due neither to accident nor to divine intervention, but to the reality of natures as secondary causes operative in the order of creation: "Accordingly we must conclude that the multitude and diversity of creatures proceeded from one principle, not on account of a necessity imposed by matter, not on account of a limitation in power, not on account of goodness or a necessity imposed by goodness, but from the order of wisdom, in order that the perfection of the universe might be realized in the diversity of creatures."[54]

KNOWLEDGE OF NATURES

Nevertheless, a nominalist might still raise the objection that, while there may be laws of nature, it is not possible to *know* them. This is indeed one of the common objections to the natural law, for as one scholar notes, "The belief that one has a determinate nature makes the injunction to live in accordance with it imperative…. The problem is thus not merely whether one has a nature of this kind, but whether it can be known."[55] This sort of skepticism about natures is in fact a widespread assumption of modern thought inspired by this seminal passage from Hume: "It must certainly be allowed, that nature has kept us at a great distance from all her secrets, and has afforded us only the knowledge of a few superficial qualities of objects; while she conceals from us those powers and principles on which the influence of those objects entirely depends."[56] On this reasoning, every individual substance, for all we know, is radically unique, and so we can never know any laws of the natural world. If true, this assumption would negate the force of my argument and leave us without knowledge of an order indicative of perfective flourishing. Once again, however, it is Thomas's metaphysics of being that will justify our knowledge of the laws of nature: the transcendental convertibility of being and thing identifies individuals with natures, and from this it can be known that there is a moral responsibility to respect the order of nature.

In his derivation of the transcendental properties, Thomas argues that certain properties belong to all beings, and so are universally predicable, *transcending* all categorical distinctions that separate different kinds of beings from one another. These properties are obtained by considering how a being must be in itself (*one*, since a divided being would be two entities, and *thing*, since every being must be of some nature), and as related to other beings. (It is an individual, this thing as opposed to that one; and inasmuch as it can be known as existent and desired for its perfection, it is *true* and *good*.) The point is that, contrary to the nominalism of the skeptics, an entity can never be a bare datum; rather, it is of necessity a being of determinate mode, and therefore having definite relations to others. It is these concomitant transcendental properties that follow upon the presence of an entity that give order and value to the universe, thereby escaping the skepticism of modernity.

This refutation of skeptical assumptions relies particularly on the clear distinction between the notion of *thing* from the notion of *being*[57] based on the real distinction between essence and existence: "The term *thing* [is derived] from the quiddity only; but the term *being* is derived from the act of being."[58] *Res* and *ens*, a thing and a being, are not strictly synonymous, but as transcendental properties are notionally distinct. The distinction here, as Jan Aertsen has argued,[59] is that the notion of thing indicates a fixed and stable essence that is a determinate mode of being, while being is the actuality of the thing itself, which gives it the intelligibility of act.[60] Thus, the intelligibility of diverse natures is grounded in the fact that the act of existence—being—manifests itself as things—individuals with determinate essences reflecting a specific mode of existence.

Yet, if this is true, then it seems that the nominalist presupposition must be wrong; we do not know radically individual beings; rather, in knowing any entity, we simultaneously know that entity as a kind of thing, a mode of existence whose activity manifests its essence.[61] Thus, any sustained observation of a being will reveal the nature of the thing; in this way mankind discerns the unique teleological vocation of each nature and the intelligible order of the world as a whole.

The convertibility of the transcendentals grounds two further points of significance: first, that these natures are conformable to the mind as true; second, that there is a moral imperative to attain the good, or perfection, of these natures that is implicit in that knowledge. As Thomas says, "Now the intellect apprehends primarily being itself; secondly, it apprehends that it understands being; and thirdly, it apprehends that it desires being. Hence the idea of being is first, that of truth second, and the idea of good third."[62] It is this unity of nature, truth, and goodness in creation that underlies Francis's call to respect nature.

First, Thomas insists that any existent thing is inherently knowable. This is because *truth* is defined as being related to mind or, more specifically, the adequation of mind and *thing*.[63] This definition avoids the problems of idealism by demanding respect for the fact of intentionality: the intelligibility of being does not start with mind alone, with man as one abstractly capable of knowing; rather, it starts with the presence of *things* in the mind, since mind is oriented to being as intelligible.[64] Indeed, this presence of things in the mind necessarily communicates both the intelligibility of the act of existence and the necessary delimitation of that act to a determinate essence. The justification of knowledge, then, relies not on man, but on the fact of the intelligible beings as ordered by God in the act of creation.

But if we can know what things are, we also know what they do, since the order of being includes the fact that action follows from being. As mentioned above, the good is the perfection of being; it is the activity which completes the nature.[65] Every nature has an inherent inclination to act in its determinate fashion. The good for that nature is the state of perfected development to which it is inclined by this natural dynamism.[66] Yet, because man knows natures, this idea of good involves man in a special way: the human will desires not just that which perfects the agent, but the universal good, that which is good in itself.[67] That ultimately is the perfection of the universe. It is for this reason that the natural law has environmental implications.

LAUDATO SI' AND STEWARDSHIP OF NATURE

To recapitulate what has been established: There is a necessary order in creation; this is not just in the ladder of being, but also in the fact that each nature is ordered to a determinate activity for the perfection of the universe. It is also true that in knowing being, we know these natures and the activities that follow from them. Lastly, we understand that these activities are perfections of that determinate nature, and necessary for the perfection of the universe.[68] Because God created each nature to attain a certain perfective activity, any order between natural things exists for the order of the whole.[69] As Olivia Blanchette explains, "The perfection of the universe does not consist in its being merely a static container of all bodies, but rather in the action and interaction of all its parts, in what could only be referred to as the order of nature."[70] Thus, each entity is called to attain its perfection, but good is diffusive and so is shared with other beings. The result of this symbiosis is the perfection of the universe. On the other hand, failure to act is a deficiency and contrary to the perfection both of the individual and of the universe.

This brings us back to natural law and the teaching of *Laudato Si'*. The natural law is simply man's rational grasp of this created ontological ordering of providence; as Thomas puts it, it is a rational creature's participation in the eternal law:

> It is evident that all things partake somewhat of the eternal law, in so far as, namely, from its being imprinted on them, they derive their respective inclinations to their proper acts and ends. Now among all others, the rational creature is subject to Divine providence in the most excellent way, in so far as it partakes of a share of providence, by being provident both for itself and for others. Wherefore it has a share of the Eternal Reason, whereby it has a natural inclination to its proper act and end: and this participation of the eternal law in the rational creature is called the natural law.[71]

The natural law enables man to understand the providential ordering of natures to their perfective activity. This is primarily concerned with acting for the perfection of human nature—to be provident for oneself by attaining happiness in terms of the rational perfections of virtue and wisdom. However, virtue and wisdom entail being provident for other creatures so as to order them to the perfection of the universe. There is, then, an isomorphism between reason's growing in understanding and man's acting for the perfection of nature: "Now the principles of reason are those things that are according to nature, because reason presupposes things as determined by nature, before disposing of other things according as it is fitting."[72] Vivian Boland succinctly comments on the unique place of the rational creature: "The privilege of the intelligent creature, Saint Thomas says, is to be capable of seeing the intelligence and goodness with which the Word of God has established the creation and which the Word has given to the creation.... If the rational creature knows something of this order in creation, he also has some responsibility for the destiny of creation."[73] The natural law directs man to grow in wisdom and love; these, in turn, demand respect for the order of nature.

This is precisely what the integral ecology of *Laudato Si'* exhorts. It urges man to not reduce reason to technological manipulation of nature to satisfy whims, but rather to respect the order of nature as God created it, and which is necessary for the perfection of the universe.[74] This means that we first of all reject modern utopian illusions that human nature itself is infinitely plastic: "Human ecology also implies another profound reality: the relationship between human life and the moral law, which is inscribed in our nature and is necessary for the creation of a more dignified environment.... It is enough to recognize that our body itself establishes us in a direct relationship with the environment and with other living beings."[75] Only once we respect the rationality of human nature can we fulfill man's unique vocation to provide providential stewardship for the rest of creation.[76] Because man has this rational capacity, he has been given a unique place in the universe: God works through secondary causes, so some created beings can be given the care of other creatures below them.[77] Since man alone has an understanding of this natural law, he has a special responsibility to order the material world in accordance with that law. So man's concern is not just his own welfare, but the welfare of creation. In other words, man has, as part of the natural law, a unique *stewardship* over creation.

Being rational thus means respecting the goodness of the order of nature, and so (quoting St. John Paul II), Francis concludes, "Any legitimate intervention will act on nature only in order 'to favour its development in its own line, that of creation, as intended by God.'"[78] Stephen Brock sees this grasping of the order of nature according to the Creator's intention as the heart of the natural law: "Natural things contain our intellect's proper object—their whatness or nature—and this is nothing other than a conception of the divine art instilled in things. And so the works of the supreme artist are to us the first and supremely intelligible things. The human artist is the one who succeeds in harnessing that primordial intelligibility."[79] This is clearly not calling on man to leave the environment alone; rather it is man's vocation to perfect nature according to reason's understanding of the eternal law. Most importantly, this ordering of nature to perfection is not primarily about the environment, for "we need to see that what is at stake is our own dignity." What is called for is interior conversion respecting both reason and the eternal law as the measure of man's own humanity and his stewardship of the environment.[80]

We are today faced with the same choice as our parents in Eden. Either we accept the goodness of the world as created, or we impose our own values upon it. As Francis points out, there can be no clearer repudiation of God's sovereignty as Lord of creation than to err in this choice: "If we approach nature and the environment without this openness to awe and wonder, if we no longer speak the language of fraternity and beauty in our relationship with the world, our attitude will be that of masters, consumers, ruthless exploiters, unable to set limits on their immediate needs."[81] We cannot escape this fact, for to ignore the reality of things and pursue our desires instead can only lead to both the diminution of human nature and the subsequent destruction of the natural world.

NOTES

1. Pope Francis, *Laudato Si'*, May 24, 2015, no. 6 (henceforth, LS). For the damage done to the environment, see no. 33; for the damage done to society, see no. 46.
2. See Pope John Paul II, *Veritatis Splendor*, August 6, 1993, no. 32.
3. For an elaboration of nominalism's role in shaping modernity, see Michael Allen Gillespie, *The Theological Origins of Modernity* (Chicago: University of Chicago Press, 2008) and Brad S. Gregory, *The Unintended Reformation* (Cambridge, MA: Belknap Press of Harvard University Press, 2012).
4. See *LS*, no. 107: "It can be said that many problems of today's world stem from the tendency, at times unconscious, to make the method and aims of science and technology an epistemological paradigm which shapes the lives of individuals and the workings of society. The effects of imposing this model on reality as a whole, human and social, are seen in the deterioration of the environment, but this is just one sign of a reductionism which affects every aspect of human and social life."
5. *LS*, no. 68: "This responsibility for God's earth means that human beings, endowed with intelligence, must respect the laws of nature."
6. See *Summa Contra Gentiles* I.1.1 and *Summa Theologiae* I.1.6 .
7. To make my argument clear, I restrict "laws of nature" to the teleological regularity of all beings as ordered to specific activities as a final cause. On the other hand, "natural law" will refer to man's rational grasp of this teleological orientation to the good as directive of action, especially with regard to human nature's own dynamic inclinations, but which also includes man's fruitful use of other creatures as a necessary means to perfection.
8. Indeed, Hilary Putnam argues that to explain the regularity nature *without* real essences would require some sort of miracle; see the discussion in Edward Feser, *Scholastic Metaphysics: A Contemporary Introduction* (Heusenstamm: Editiones Scholasticae, 2014), 212-213. Good illustrations of the inductive argument for metaphysical realism from our experience of nature are found in James Ross, *Thought and World* (Notre Dame, IN: University of Notre Dame Press, 2008), and David S. Oderberg, *Real Essentialism* (New York: Routledge, 2007); for an example of this method applied to natural law ethics, see Steven J. Jensen, *Knowing the Natural Law: From Precepts and Inclinations to Deriving Oughts* (Washington: The Catholic University of America Press, 2015).
9. See also the well-developed parallel in *De Potentia* 3.16.
10. *Summa Contra Gentiles* III.97.15 (henceforth, *SCG*; all citations are taken from the translation in four volumes by Anton C. Pegis, James F. Anderson, Vernon J. Bourke, and Charles O'Neil [Notre Dame, IN: University of Notre Dame Press, 1975]).
11. Of course, not all Islamic philosophers were divine voluntarists; however, by the start of the Thirteenth Century, the voluntarist Asherite school had

gained a decisive ascendancy over the Mutazalite school, and their position has been the *de facto* orthodoxy of Islam ever since. On this, see Robert R. Reilly, *The Closing of the Muslim Mind* (Wilmington, DE: ISI Books, 2010).

12. In *SCG* III.97.11, Thomas concludes by pointing out that this order requires the numerical plurality of creatures to represent God's goodness: "Therefore, just as the first rational principle of divine providence is simply the divine goodness, so the first rational principle in creatures is their numerical plurality, to the establishment and conservation of which all other things seem to be ordered."
13. *SCG* III.97.2.
14. *Summa Theologica* I.19.3 (henceforth, *ST*; all citations taken from the translation by the Fathers of the English Dominican Province [New York: Benzinger, 1948; reprint, Allen, TX: Christian Classics, 1981]).
15. *ST* I.19.2. Thomas is here adapting for his purposes the Dionysian idea that the good is self-diffusive; see Fran O'Rourke, *Pseudo-Dionysius and the Metaphysics of Aquinas* (Notre Dame, IN: University of Notre Dame Press, 1992), 215-274.
16. Unlike a finite creature's power, which is determined to one specific effect, God's infinite nature accounts for all *possible* effects; see SCG II.23.
17. *De Potentia* 1.5: "Now the natural end of the divine will is the divine goodness, which it is unable not to will. Creatures, however, are not proportionate to this end, as though without them the divine goodness could not be made manifest, which manifestation was God's intention in creating. For even as the divine goodness is made manifest through these things that are and through this order of things, so could it be made manifest through other creatures and another order." All citations to *De Potentia* (henceforth, *DP*) are taken from *On the Power of God*, translated by the English Dominican Fathers (Westminster, MD: Newman Press, 1952). Cf. ST I.19.3 and I.19.5.
18. *De Veritate* 1.1.
19. *ST* I.5.1: "The essence of goodness consists in this that it is in some way desirable.... Now it is clear that a thing is desirable only in so far as it is perfect; for all desire their own perfection. But everything is perfect so far as it is actual. Therefore it is clear that a thing is perfect so far as it exists; for it is existence that makes all things actual."
20. *ST* I.4.2; cf. *DP* 1.2 and *ST* I.13.11.
21. See *ST* I.45.1 and 5; this implies that creatures must always be preserved by God (*ST* I.104.1 and 3).
22. *ST* I.44.1; cf. *SCG* II.52.8.
23. Thomas sees this as a primary way to prove the existence of God; see *DP* 7.2; *ST* I.65.1; and *SCG* II.15-16.
24. *SCG* III.66.6-7.
25. *DP* 3.1: "Now a particular thing is actual in a particular manner.... Wherefore a natural agent produces a being not simply, but determines a pre-

existent being to this or that species.... On the other hand God is all act... because in him is the source of all things, wherefore by his action he produces the whole subsistent being." See also *ST* I.45.1-2.
26. *SCG* 97.2; see also *ST* I.47.1.
27. *DP* 7.2.ad 9; see also *ST* I.4.1.ad 3.
28. *ST* I.3.4.
29. See *DP* 4.1-2, in which Thomas makes clear that regardless of the temporal conditions of creation, it is nonetheless a single creative act of God.
30. See Vivian Boland, OP, *Ideas in God According to St. Thomas Aquinas: Sources and Synthesis* (New York: E.J. Brill, 1996).
31. *ST* I.15.2; cf. *ST* I.47.1.ad 2.
32. *ST* I.44.3.
33. *SCG* 97.3.
34. *SCG* I.43.5 and 8. See also *SCG* I.26.3 and II.52.1. For an analysis of the significance of the fact that the act of existence is not self-limiting, see Steven A. Long, *Analogia Entis: On the Analogy of Being, Metaphysics, and the Act of Faith* (Notre Dame, IN: University of Notre Dame Press, 2011), 13-37.
35. The classic statement of this argument is in *De ente et essentia,* c. 4.
36. The very fact of being created *ex nihilo* necessitates a limiting potency in all creatures: see *DP* 1.2.ad 4: "The very notion of being made or created is incompatible with the infinite. The very fact that it is made out of nothing, argues its imperfection and potentiality, and shows that it is not pure act: and consequently it cannot be equaled to the infinite, as though it also were infinite." It is for this reason that no perfection can ever be univocally attributed to God and creature (*DP* 7.7).
37. *SCG* 97.3.
38. *SCG* II.45.6; cf. *ST* I.47.2.
39. *SCG* II.45.4; cf. *ST* I.65.2: "Therefore, in the parts of the universe also every creature exists for its own proper act and perfection, and the less noble for the nobler, as those creatures that are less noble than man exist for the sake of man, whilst each and every creature exists for the perfection of the entire universe." See also ST I.103.3.
40. A related objection might be that God could create a single instance of a substance, and a single substance cannot be considered a universal. In *Commentary on Aristotle's "Metaphysics"* VII.13.1574, Thomas replies that while there can be no universal without a single instantiation, a singular nevertheless indicates that universal mode of being characteristic of all the individuals which embody it, however many there may be. See also *DP* 9.4.ad 18.
41. *ST* I.47.2; cf. *ST* I.103.1 and DP 3.16.
42. *SCG* III.97.7. From this Thomas concludes (in 9) that even the accidents of each substance are under the order of providence since they arise from this union of form and matter. That form and matter, as principles and not things, must necessarily be concreated, see *SCG* II.80-81.7, *DP* 3.1.ad 12, *ST* I. 45.4, and *ST* I.66.1.

43. See *De Ente et Essentia* c. 2.
44. *SCG* II.68.3. See also *De ente et essentia*, c.5, in which Thomas discusses the "double composition" of act and potency in material substances.
45. *SCG* II.30.8.
46. *SCG* III.97.13: "If we grant that, as a result of an act of divine will, He wills to establish this particular number of things, and this definite measure of perfection for each thing, then as a result one finds the reason why each thing has a certain form and a certain kind of matter."
47. *SCG* III.97.4.
48. *SCG* II.30.9-11.
49. *ST* I.105.5. See also *SCG* III.113.1. It is this activity that is the ultimate goal of God in creating, for He creates for the active perfection of the universe that is achieved in the preservation of this causal order (see *SCG* III.69.16-18), but this causal order is itself directed to the perfection of the creation in terms of man's fulfillment in the beatific vision (*ST* I.73.1).
50. *ST* I.22.3: "[God] governs things inferior by superior, not on account of any defect in His power, but by reason of the abundance of His goodness; so that the dignity of causality is imparted even to creatures." See also *SCG* III.77, esp. 3.
51. *DP* 3.7.ad 16. See also *ST* I.19.5.ad 2: "Since God wills effects to proceed from definite causes, for the preservation of order in the universe, it is not unreasonable to seek for causes secondary to the divine will."
52. See prologue to *ST* I.44.
53. See *ST* I.25.3, where Thomas explains "that which implies being and non-being at the same time is repugnant to the idea of an absolutely possible thing." See also *SCG* II.22.3 and *DP* I.7. On the notion that omnipotence must be understood not as an abstract absolute, but rather in relation to the divine nature, see Louis Groarke, "Reconsidering Absolute Omnipotence," *Heythrop Journal* XLII (2001), 13-25.
54. *DP* 3.16.
55. Stephen Buckle, cited in Howard Kainz, *Natural Law: An Introduction and Re-examination* (Chicago and La Salle, IL: Open Court, 2004), 115.
56. David Hume, *Enquiry Concerning Human Understanding*, ed. by L.A. Selby-Bigge, 3rd edition (Oxford: Clarendon Press, 1975), Sec. IV, part ii, 32-33.
57. See *De Veritate* 1.1; cf. *ST* I. 39.3.ad 3. I acknowledge, but do not here develop, the related relevance of the transcendental *aliquid*, or something, which represents the individuality of beings.
58. *Commentary on the Metaphysics* IV.2.553 (translated by John P. Rowan [Notre Dame, IN: Dumb Ox Books, 1995]).
59. Jan Aertsen, *Medieval Philosophy and the Transcendentals: The Case of Thomas Aquinas* (Leiden: E.J. Brill, 1996), 193-200.
60. See *ST* I.5.2: "Now the first thing conceived by the intellect is being;

because everything is knowable only inasmuch as it is in actuality. Hence, being is the proper object of the intellect, and is primarily intelligible."
61. See Norris Clarke, SJ, "Action as the Self-Revelation of Being: A Central Theme in the Thought of St. Thomas" in *Explorations in Metaphysics: Being, God, Person* (Notre Dame, IN: University of Notre Dame Press, 1995), 45-64.
62. *ST* I.16.4.ad 2.
63. *De Veritate* 1.1; see also ST I.15.1. The grounding of truth in being, as opposed to subjective consciousness, avoids the circularity of modern epistemology's "problem of the criterion" (see Roderick Chisholm, *The Problem of the Criterion* (Milwaukee: Marquette University Press, 1973)), in which truth is defined by reference to either what we know or the method by which we know it, since whichever one chooses, that foundation will ultimately be arbitrary. On the necessary priority of metaphysics over epistemology, see Feser, *Scholastic Metaphysics*, 27-28.
64. *ST* I.85.6; see Stephen L. Brock, *The Philosophy of Saint Thomas Aquinas: A Sketch* (Eugene, OR: Cascade Books, 2015), 85-103.
65. *ST* I.5.1.ad.1.
66. Thus, Stephen Brock points out the fecklessness of Hume's argument for the fact-value dichotomy: it is not that nature implies good, but that good implies nature as perfected; see "Natural Inclination and the Intelligibility of the Good in Thomistic Natural Law," *Vera Lex* VI (2005), 57-78.
67. *SCG* II.47-48.
68. *ST* I.15.2: "In proof of which it is to be considered that in every effect the ultimate end is the proper intention of the principal agent, as order of an army (is the proper intention) of the general. Now the highest good existing in things is the good of the order of the universe.... Therefore, the order of the universe is properly intended by God, and is not the accidental result of a succession of agents."
69. *De Veritate* 5.3: "In an army we find two orders, one by which the parts of the army are related to each other, and a second by which the army is directed to an external good, namely, the good of its leader.... Consequently, if the subordination to the leader did not exist, the ordering of the parts of the army to each other would not exist. Consequently, whenever we find a group whose members are ordered to each other, that group must necessarily be ordered to some external principle" (translation from *Truth*, tr. by Robert W. Mulligan, S.J., James V. McGlynn, S.J., and Robert W. Schmidt, S.J. [Chicago: Henry Regnery, 1954; reprint, Indianapolis: Hackett, 1994]). Cf. also SCG III.64.
70. Olivia Blanchette, T*he Perfection of the Universe According to Aquinas: A Teleological Cosmology* (University Park, PA: Pennsylvania State University Press, 1992), 203.
71. *ST* I-II.91.1. Cf. I-II.93.6: "There are two ways in which a thing is subject to the eternal law: first, by partaking of the eternal law by way of knowledge;

secondly, by way of action and passion.... The rational nature...is subject to the eternal law in both ways; because each rational creature has some knowledge of the eternal law."

72. *Summa Theologiae* II-II.154.12.
73. Boland, *Ideas in God*, 327.
74. *LS* 115: "Modern anthropocentrism has paradoxically ended up prizing technical thought over reality.... The intrinsic dignity of the world is thus compromised. When human beings fail to find their true place in this world, they misunderstand themselves and end up acting against themselves."
75. *LS* 155.
76. See *LS* 139.
77. See *SCG* III.76-81, 113, and 147-148. Note that the angels, who are not material and so not directly involved in the operations of the material world, have a completely different sort of care for this material world.
78. *LS* 132.
79. Brock, *The Philosophy of Saint Thomas Aquinas*, 164.
80. *LS* 160 and 217. Blanchette makes this point lucidly: "And because there are many individual persons who have this right to use [nature], the rub is to find how the right use of each over the whole of nature is to be exercised and realized to the common benefit of all.... Only reason can establish the right that only follows from the natural order of things" (*The Perfection of the Universe*), 289.
81. *LS* 11. This attitude evokes that primordial sin, acedia, which evacuates the world of value: "The thing's authentic otherness is obscured, for when objects are forced to stand over against us before submitting to us, their interiority, goodness, and beauty are vacated.... Objects become beautiful if they please us, according to our subjective taste, rather than demanding our delight as a matter of justice; objects become good if they serve us, according to our subjective purposes, rather than demand our willing them in keeping with God's own judgment and instruction." R. J. Snell, *Acedia: Metaphysical Boredom in an Empire of Desire* (Kettering, OH: Angelico Press, 2015), 83.

LAUDATO SI': A NATURAL LAW ETHIC OF CARE

Michael Dauphinais

Pope Francis' recent encyclical, *Laudato Si'*, has been referred to as the "climate-change encyclical" or, more understandably, as the "encyclical on the environment," which nonetheless may leave readers wondering why the Pope speaks so much about morality and society.[1] I contend that a clue may be found in the subtitle of *Laudato Si'*, "On Care for Our Common Home." The encyclical's focus may be viewed from the human virtue of caring. In deliberately choosing this subtitle, Pope Francis makes the human virtue of caring the focus of *Laudato Si'*. Examining the encyclical through the hermeneutical lens of care that Pope Francis himself provides us with, we see that *Laudato Si'* possesses a strong foundation in the natural law tradition. Given this, I will both analyze the many places in the encyclical wherein Pope Francis works from this tradition and examine the symbiotic relationship of *Laudato Si'* with Thomas Aquinas's presentation of the natural law as well as C. S. Lewis's *The Abolition of Man*. In brief, I contend the central claim of *Laudato Si'* hinges on a traditional view of morality and the natural moral law. As such, the encyclical presents a powerful critique of the reductionistic and relativistic tendencies within contemporary society and provides a viable solution to the ethical crises of our age through what I call—hewing to the encyclical's subtitle—Pope Francis's "natural law ethic of care."

What exactly does the verb "to care for" mean in English? The *Oxford English Dictionary* lists this as the third meaning of "care": "to take thought for, provide for, look after, take care of."[2] "Care" indicates concern for the well-being of another and is typically associated with protection.[3] Care can be seen more clearly in its similarity to—and difference from—friendship. Following

Aristotle, Aquinas said that friendship was constituted by benevolence, desiring the good of the other for the sake of the other. Friendship distinctively indicates a kind of equality and communication. Aquinas said that love (*caritas*) is friendship with God, which is only possible because through the Incarnation we have become "sharers in the divine nature."[4] Even so, God remains ever greater than the human creature, who is ever in need of his protection; as First Peter instructs, "Cast all your anxieties on God, for he *cares* about you."[5] Care thus demands no equality, but even thrives on inequality, we might say, whether this inequality arises from the difference in the natures of the parties or from the differences of circumstances whereby we see the other as in need of assistance and worthy of assistance. In this sense, animals may live in harmony with their environment and may be said to care for their young, but they cannot properly be said to have the virtue of care in the sense we are using it here. In this context, care is a distinctive human virtue that requires a rational apprehension of the needs and nature of the other person and of the non-human environment. Therefore, when Pope Francis speaks of caring for our common home in the subtitle of *Laudato Si'*, he focuses on developing the uniquely human ability to care for other people and our common environment by recognizing the interrelated character of the natural environment, human beings, and their common Creator.[6]

The language of care and caring pervades the encyclical and is not limited to its subtitle. Pope Francis explicitly connects his namesake, St. Francis of Assisi, whose hymn *Laudato Si'* forms the title of the encyclical, to the care for creation: "[St. Francis of Assisi] felt called to care for all that exists."[7] The initial invitation of the encyclical is summarized with the language of care: "[all] of us can cooperate as instruments of God for the *care* of creation, each according to his or her own culture, experience, involvements and talents."[8] Here Pope Francis explicitly situates care within an account of creation and the human recognition of the Creator. Elsewhere he underscores that this theistic dimension widens the ambit of care to include not only the natural environment but also the poor: "I would like from the outset to show how faith convictions can offer Christians, and some other believers as well, ample motivation to *care* for nature and for the most vulnerable of their brothers and sisters."[9] The Pope frames this ethic of care as the alternative to the disordered exaltation of power: "If we acknowledge the value and the fragility of nature and, at the same time, our God-given abilities, we can finally leave behind the modern myth of unlimited material progress. A fragile world, entrusted by God to human *care*, challenges us to devise intelligent ways of directing, developing and limiting our power." In sum, in *Laudato Si'* Pope Francis is calling for a human *ethos* of care—theistically grounded—to supplant the regnant *mythos* of unbridled materialism and the insatiable thirst for power.[10]

In this article I will elucidate the encyclical's teaching on care for our common home and the principles necessary to receive that teaching. First, it begins by addressing the way in which Pope Francis consistently resituates discussions about the environment within considerations about the moral dimensions of human society. Second, it examines the recurring criticisms of the reductionist technocratic paradigms that dominate modern thought and society. Third, the article turns to C. S. Lewis's *The Abolition of Man* to consider the correspondence between the reduction of the natural world and the reduction of the moral world and then, fourth, to Thomas Aquinas's presentation of the natural law to show its necessity for coherent thinking about the virtue of care. Fifth and finally, the article considers why the technocratic and relativistic commitments of much of the present age weaken the very ability to inculcate the virtues of care and charity that are necessary to assist in the cultivation of human and natural environments.

LAUDATO SI': A SOCIAL ENCYCLICAL ON THE ENVIRONMENT OR AN ENVIRONMENTAL ENCYCLICAL ON SOCIETY?

The encyclical addresses the concern for the natural environment in the midst of concern for the social environment of human beings. By drawing frequent parallels between the environmental crises and the societal crises of the modern age, the encyclical emphasizes that any solution to the problems currently affecting the environment must flow from changes in the way human beings interact with one another: in other words, from a recovery of a moral dimension of human society. Pope Francis calls forth continuity with the teaching of Pope Benedict XVI at the beginning of this encyclical on this very interconnection: "He observed that the world cannot be analyzed by isolating only one of its aspects, since 'the book of nature is one and indivisible,' and includes the environment, life, sexuality, the family, social relations, and so forth. It follows that 'the deterioration of nature is closely connected to the culture which shapes human coexistence.'"[11] The importance of this theme can be seen from the sheer number of quotes that establish the environmental situation within the broader societal and moral condition:

> If the present ecological crisis is one small sign of the ethical, cultural and spiritual crisis of modernity, we cannot presume to heal our relationship with nature and the environment without healing all fundamental human relationships.[12]
>
> When we speak of the "environment," what we really mean is a relationship existing between nature and the society which lives in it.[13]
>
> If everything is related, then the health of a society's institutions has consequences for the environment and the quality of human life.[14]
>
> Our difficulty in taking up this challenge seriously has much to do with an ethical and cultural decline which has accompanied the deterioration of the environment.[15]
>
> [St. Francis of Assisi] shows us just how inseparable the bond is between concern for nature, justice for the poor, commitment to society, and interior peace.[16]

If the reader were to imagine a Venn diagram, the larger circle of the social and moral situation would encompass the smaller circle of the ecological issues. This implies a profound reframing of the contemporary concern for the degradation of the environment. It is not sufficient to protect the natural environment from human interference. In fact, this would not be properly human. Instead, the concern for the natural environment can never be separated from the concern for other people. Human beings possess a vocation to live, to live with each other, and to live within the environment.

Pope Francis frames the interrelation of the natural and social environments with a beautiful expression: "a culture of care." Care for nature falls thus within the need to love our neighbor at the personal, civic, and political levels.[17] Pope Francis writes, "In this framework, along with the importance of little everyday gestures, social love moves us to devise larger strategies to halt environmental degradation and to encourage a *'culture of care'* which permeates all of society."[18] The renewal of this culture of care is the social call of the encyclical. The culture of care necessitates deep interior conversion in which the needs of our neighbor and our environment are received: "Disinterested concern for others, and the rejection of every form of self-centeredness and self-absorption, are essential if we truly wish to *care* for our brothers and sisters and for the natural environment."[19]

The importance of care within the encyclical can be seen in some of its closing exhortations. Mary and Joseph are adduced as exemplars of this ethic of care: "Mary, the Mother who *cared* for Jesus, now *cares* with maternal affection and pain for this wounded world."[20] As for Joseph, "Through his work and generous presence, he *cared* for and defended Mary and Jesus, delivering them from the violence of the unjust by bringing them to Egypt."[21] In particular, Joseph is a model of caring, one from whom we are invited to learn and to imitate: "He too can teach us how to show *care*; he can inspire us to work with generosity and tenderness in protecting this world which God has entrusted to us."[22] Human work is not merely a technical activity, but has a properly human dimension that may express a care for others and a care for the broader environment.

Even in the practical recommendations from the encyclical, the language of care remains prevalent. Such language thus serves as an implicit reminder of the moral foundations of protection of the natural environment and concern for the poor: "The 1992 Earth Summit in Rio de Janeiro is worth mentioning. It proclaimed that 'human beings are at the centre of concerns for sustainable development.' Echoing the 1972 Stockholm Declaration, it enshrined international cooperation to *care* for the ecosystem of the entire earth, the obligation of those who cause pollution to assume its costs, and the duty to assess the environmental impact of given projects and works."[23] The encyclical consistently unites the dual-preservation of the natural and the human social and moral environments through the language of care.

LAUDATO SI' AND THE TWIN DANGERS OF TECHNOCRACY AND BIOCENTRISM

In *Laudato Si'*, Pope Francis warns of twin dangers at the root of the present environmental crisis: a technological paradigm that only seeks to exploit the environment and a biological paradigm that seeks to deny human uniqueness. These may be seen as the Scylla and Charybdis of the contemporary environmental movement. The technocratic paradigm, pervasive in modernity, undermines care for the environment with the myth of limitless power over the natural world. "Biocentricism," as labeled in the encyclical, is the strand within environmentalism that denies human uniqueness in order to argue that human beings should no longer be viewed as having a special role in the environment.[24] Somehow, according to this view, once bereft of a special role, human beings will then act unlike other creatures and no longer struggle to survive and to reproduce. These relativisitic strands within environmentalism eschew references to objective morality since such morality often functions as an obstacle to population control and widespread adoption of contraception and abortion. The technocratic paradigm implicitly entails the biocentric denial of the uniqueness of the human race since it treats all of the known world, including human beings, as objects for technical manipulation.

Care for the environment becomes impossible if human beings treat things as mere objects to be manipulated at will, the *modus operandi* of a technocracy. The Pope cautions, "humanity has taken up technology and its development according to an undifferentiated and one-dimensional paradigm. This paradigm exalts the concept of a subject who, using logical and rational procedures, progressively approaches and gains control over an external object."[25] The Pope here contrasts care for the environment and the one-dimensional paradigm of the modern subject exerting power over external objects. To care about someone or for something recognizes that the recipient of such care has an order of its own that demands respect, and so the virtue of caring differs not only from the technocratic paradigm but also from the biocentric view:

> Christian thought sees human beings as possessing a particular dignity above other creatures; it thus inculcates esteem for each person and respect for others. Our openness to others, each of whom is a 'thou' capable of knowing, loving and entering into dialogue, remains the source of our nobility as human persons. A correct relationship with the created world demands that we not weaken this social dimension of openness to others, much less the transcendent dimension of our openness to the 'Thou' of God. Our relationship with the environment can never be isolated from our relationship with others and with God.[26]

This is a crucial point since it shows that one should not discuss environmental issues without paying attention to the nature of the human person who is discussing those environmental issues. What is the nature of the human person? If we cannot discuss this idea with any sense of meaning or consensus, we will certainly fail to have consensus on the nature of the non-human environment. This is why the encyclical presents the human person as a subject capable of entering into relationships with other subjects and, ultimately, with the divine other of God. For Pope Francis, anthropology is ineluctably tied to theology. The encyclical observes that contemporary thinkers often fail to recognize the importance of just societal interactions:

> And yet, when there is a general breakdown in the exercise of a certain virtue in personal and social life, it ends up causing a number of imbalances, including environmental ones. That is why it is no longer enough to speak only of the integrity of ecosystems. We have to dare to speak of the integrity of human life, of the need to promote and unify all the great

values. Once we lose our humility, and become enthralled with the possibility of limitless mastery over everything, we inevitably end up harming society and the environment.[27]

The concern for the environment thus necessitates a consideration of foundational human virtues and values. *Laudato Si'* makes this connection explicit: "The effects of imposing this model [of the technocratic paradigm] on reality as a whole, human and social, are seen in the deterioration of the environment, but this is just one sign of a reductionism which affects every aspect of human and social life."[28]

The order present in natural beings and in the environment as a whole places limits on human action.[29] Yet, these constraints are exactly what the technological paradigm denies. All is available for research; all must bend beneath the human will. The Pope connects exploitation of the environment to exploitation of human beings as examples of "a disregard for the message contained in the structures of nature itself. When we fail to acknowledge as part of reality the worth of a poor person, a human embryo, a person with disabilities – to offer just a few examples – it becomes difficult to hear the cry of nature itself; everything is connected."[30] A meaningful call to care for the environment must include a recognition of its inner structures and even more so the objective dignity of human beings that demand a certain kind of care. Here the rejection of the technocratic paradigm leads to a rejection of the biocentricism that fails to see each person's worth and responsibility. Proper care is not license: "[I]t is troubling that, when some ecological movements defend the integrity of the environment, rightly demanding that certain limits be imposed on scientific research, they sometimes fail to apply those same principles to human life. There is a tendency to justify transgressing all boundaries when experimentation is carried out on living human embryos."[31] Recovering the virtue of care requires recognizing the nature of each thing or person before us and the inherent worth in that thing or person that places limits on how we might use or interact with that reality. The encyclical tends to avoid an overly abstract consideration of these principles and instead uses images such as the exploitation of children, the elderly, the poor, the physically disabled, and the unborn as aids to awaken consciences.³²

The encyclical calls not only for a commitment to the care of our common home, but also for a recognition of the kind of creature who is capable of caring. To care requires the ability to recognize the other as other, yet also to feel responsibility towards the other, and finally to see the other's inner worth and order. Here Pope Francis challenges one of the central dogmas of contemporary environmentalism, namely, that environmental degradation stems from the myth of human uniqueness and so must be combated by putting human beings on the same level as the rest of our environment. He writes, "Human beings, even if we postulate a process of evolution, also possess a uniqueness which cannot be fully explained by the evolution of other open systems. ... The biblical accounts of creation invite us to see each human being as a subject who can never be reduced to the status of an object."³³ The call to care for the environment is only possible if human beings are seen as unique in their moral responsibility: "This rediscovery of nature can never be at the cost of the freedom and responsibility of human beings who, as part of the world, have the duty to cultivate their abilities in order to protect it and develop its potential."³⁴ Only humans may be said to care for the environment.

It is not accidental, however, that the modern technological paradigm, and its concomitant undermining of the uniqueness of human beings, also undermines moral truths. Pope Francis writes, "Human ecology also implies another profound reality: the relationship between human life and the moral law, which is inscribed in our nature and is necessary for the creation of a more dignified environment." He then quotes Pope Benedict XVI, who "spoke of an 'ecology of man,' based on the fact that 'man too has a nature that he must respect and that he cannot manipulate at will.'"³⁵ Such manipulation is seen most clearly in abortion, when more powerful human beings end the life of the less powerful. This is why the references to embryos and abortion are not extraneous to the encyclical.³⁶ Abortion is the fruit of the technological paradigm applied to human beings themselves. Pope Francis writes, "Our difficulty in taking up this challenge seriously has much to do with an ethical and cultural decline which has accompanied the deterioration of the environment."[37] One cannot fix the problems of how human beings treat the environment without addressing the problems of how we treat one another.

Pope Francis draws on a tradition of papal teachings in which modern crises of technology, war, and society are traced back to fundamental errors in the understanding of the human person. In particular, Pope Paul VI's encyclical *Populorum Progressio* highlighted this critique of the technocratic paradigm.[38] To speak of technocracy is not to address technology per se, but rather to emphasize the danger of allowing technological development to cloud over moral concerns about the human person. Paul VI argues that the ultimate purpose of all societal development must have one aim: "to serve human nature."[39] This requires a robust understanding of human nature and its moral dimension prior to concerns for improving productivity of economic systems. Here is how Paul VI diagnoses what he terms "the reign of technology" or "technocracy":

> The reign of technology—technocracy, as it is called—can cause as much harm to the world of tomorrow as liberalism did to the world of yesteryear. Economics and technology are meaningless if they do not benefit man, for it is he they are to serve. Man is truly human only if he is the master of his own actions and the judge of their worth, only if he is the architect of his own progress. He must act according to his God-given nature, freely accepting its potentials and its claims upon him.[40]

With this central critique, Pope Paul VI embraced the good of societal and economic development by turning it on its head. He clearly states that human nature acts as the guiding principle for true development. Human nature is something "God-given" with specific "potentials" and "claims."

Paul VI's critique becomes more easily understood when we consider its converse. If technology does not serve human nature, then human nature serves technology. This means that technology then operates upon human nature as it does on raw material. More precisely, some human beings who possess more power and more technology exploit those human beings with less power.

RELATIVISM UNVEILED:
C. S. LEWIS AND *LAUDATO SI'*

C. S. Lewis, in his justly famous *The Abolition of Man* (1943), wrote that "Man's conquest of Nature turns out, in the moment of its consummation, to be Nature's conquest of Man."[41] Lewis observes a dynamic in which human beings approach themselves in the same manner in which they approach the rest of nature. In particular, Lewis expressed a two-fold concern, bringing together two strands of thought often unconnected: moral relativism and the technological conquest of nature.[42]

Lewis argued that when the modern movement set aside objective moral value, it decisively broke with traditionally understood notions of what it means to be human. When moral truth is expunged, then there are no longer proper or improper emotional responses to the world around us; there are merely responses to stimuli. Without objective moral responses, only scientific, or calculating, reason remains to guide human action. The traditional notion, expressed already in Plato, was that the human reason governs the appetites through the emotions or "spirited nature." In Lewis's apt turn of phrase, "The head rules the belly through the chest."[43] Instead, Lewis saw modern education producing "men without chests," i.e., bellies and brains without hearts and values, leading to technical exploitation of human beings and the environment. The traditional view exalted the garden, in which human beings cultivated nature for the purpose of beauty and enjoyment; the modern view either wishes nature to be left as a wilderness or exploited for wealth.

Lewis diagnoses relativism not as an advance forward beyond more primitive notions of right and wrong; rather, relativism takes away that peculiar moral note that has been the human contribution to the symphony—and cacophony—of creation. He writes, "Nature will be troubled no more by the restive species that rose in revolt against her so many millions of years ago, will be vexed no longer by its chatter of truth and mercy and beauty and happiness."[44] The attempt to unshackle themselves from traditional morality has reduced human beings to the realm of the sub-human. As Lewis summarizes so eloquently, "The real objection is that if man chooses to treat himself as raw material, raw material he will be: not raw material to be manipulated, as he fondly imagined, by himself, but by mere appetite, that is, mere Nature, in the person of his dehumanized Conditioners."[45]

In a similar move, *Laudato Si'* does not simply critique relativism as false, but shows that it is a degradation of the uniquely human ability to choose to care for those with less power than ourselves. The opposite of relativism thus is not merely an objective moral order. Instead, the opposite of relativism is the virtue of care. Relativism signifies the unrestrained exploitation of the weaker by the stronger, first among human beings and then of human beings over the natural environment: "The culture of relativism is the same disorder which drives one person to take advantage of another, to treat others as mere objects, imposing forced labour on them or enslaving them to pay their debts. The same kind of thinking leads to the sexual exploitation of children and abandonment of the elderly who no longer serve our interests."[46] *Laudato Si'* critiques the comfortable relativism of the elites and powerful who may impose their will on others by unveiling its effect on the poor, children, and the elderly. Pope Francis specifically challenges the culture of relativism and names its uglier manifestations. For instance, he writes, "Is it not the same relativistic logic which justifies buying the organs of the poor for resale or use in experimentation, or eliminating children because they are not what their parents wanted?"[47] Contrary to a dominant view within the contemporary societies of the West, relativism does not lead to the liberty of the individual, but to the exploitation of weaker individuals and the environment at the hands of the more powerful.

The encyclical is not content to criticize relativism without presenting a compelling alternative. The opposite of relativism is personified in the life of St. Francis of Assisi, who not only listened to the song of the birds and thus appreciated the environment, but also kissed the lepers, the poorest of the poor in his society: "I believe that Saint Francis is the example par excellence of *care* for the vulnerable and of an integral ecology lived out joyfully and authentically."[48] The encyclical presents Francis of Assisi, not as an anti-technological or anti-human environmentalist, but as a model of the holistic and ordered love for God, human beings, and non-human creation. Pope Francis defends the necessity of this holistic love: "Our relationship with the environment can never be isolated from our relationship with others and with God. Otherwise, it would be nothing more than romantic individualism dressed up in ecological garb, locking us into a stifling immanence."[49] Thus, the encyclical eschews the anti-theistic romanticizing of undeveloped nature with which Francis of Assisi is oftentimes viewed in the contemporary culture of the West.

NATURAL LAW AND INTEGRAL ECOLOGY

The term "natural law" is admittedly not found in *Laudato Si'*. The terms "moral law" and "moral structure" are both only used once.[50] So the reader might ask how my emphasis on the natural law is justified. The appropriateness of this language stems from its opposition to the technocratic paradigm, which is above all a reduction of the human person from a moral structure with inherent limits and dignity to an object of unlimited plasticity subject to the technological manipulation of the powerful.

A brief presentation of Thomas Aquinas's discussion of natural law reveals significant continuity with some of the key ideas of the encyclical. Without delving into the many complexities of Aquinas's sophisticated and multi-layered presentation of the natural moral law, two foundational points may be observed. First, the natural law begins as the necessary mode of moral reasoning and acting by the human being. Human action is not random, but is pursued intelligibly by acting for the sake of some perceived good or desirable purpose.[51] This fundamental inclination to the good leads to the primary precept of the natural law: "good is to be done and pursued, and evil is to be avoided."[52] Second, out of this fundamental inclination and precept, there are three further inclinations as understood from reason. From the inclination to the good of one's own being comes the inclination toward preservation of one's own life. From the inclination to the good of sex and offspring comes the inclination to sexual intercourse and the education of offspring. From the inclination to seek the good in accord with reason comes the "natural inclination to know the truth about God and to live in society."[53] Although Aquinas distinguishes the above in a three-part schema, it helps the present purpose to split up the last part to have a four-part schema: self-preservation, preservation of human life through the family, preservation of societal life, and preservation of knowledge of God. Note that the natural inclination to know the truth about God does not need to include all that is manifested through divine revelation, but is properly focused on the natural knowledge of God as Creator that is attainable, at least in principle, according to the natural powers of the rational creature.[54] Thus the natural law concerns more than merely societal relationships, but includes all four levels of relationships, including the recognition of God.

Laudato Si' frequently refers to these four levels of natural law inclinations and makes explicit the connection to the natural environment. As was shown earlier in this essay, *Laudato Si'* emphasizes that environmental crises are properly viewed within broader societal and moral crises. For instance, the decline of the environment is linked to the decline of society, or, conversely, the preservation of the environment is linked to the preservation of society. In this manner, the three-fold preservation of one's own life, of the life of the next generation in the family, and of life together in society all require the preservation of the natural environment in which the person, the family, and the members of society all live. Moreover, the natural law context of the act of preservation indicates that not only the natural environment must be preserved, but also the moral structures of the person, the family, and society. This holistic view of natural law assists in understanding the relationship between caring for the environment and an authentic sexuality that respects moral norms. Pope Francis writes, "Learning to accept our body, to care for it and to respect its fullest meaning, is an essential element of any genuine human ecology. Also, valuing one's own body in its femininity or masculinity is necessary if I am going to be able to recognize myself in an encounter with someone who is different."[55] Care for one's body requires a receptivity to its structures, including its embodiment as male or female. These physical structures in turn participate in the moral structures of the human person.[56] The sexual embodiment and its accompanying inclinations and precepts give concreteness to the general precept "do good and avoid evil" in the areas of the person, the family, and society. Moreover, the full background of natural law assists the reader of the encyclical to understand the many references to the need to recognize God as the Creator throughout the encyclical.

The encyclical presents the interplay of these four dimensions of the natural law through the language of an "integral ecology." This idea is introduced at the beginning of the encyclical: "Francis [of Assisi] helps us to see that an integral ecology calls for an openness to categories which transcend the language of mathematics and biology, and take us to the heart of what it is to be human."[57] The language of mathematics and biology fails to disclose the moral dimension of the human person. This moral dimension of the human person is revealed in the love of God and the love of neighbor—a love that respects the moral worth of the person as a creature laden with dignity prior to my ability to manipulate the person via technological means.

The development of the theme of integral ecology explicitly builds upon the moral law. In fact, although Pope Benedict is cited many times in this encyclical, it is the citation of his references to natural law that are of particular interest to the theme we are considering at present. Pope Francis explicitly refers to his predecessor in developing the central theme of integral ecology: "Human ecology also implies another profound reality: the relationship between human life and the moral law, which is inscribed in our nature and is necessary for the creation of a more dignified environment. Pope Benedict XVI spoke of an 'ecology of man,' based on the fact that 'man too has a nature that he must respect and that he cannot manipulate at will.'"[58] The reference to Pope Benedict here comes from an address he gave to the German Bundestad (or Lower Parliament) on the nature of law and its inherent moral dimension. Thus we can see that when Pope Francis refers to an "ecology of man" or speaks of an "integral ecology," he is reaffirming the traditional notion of natural law in a context that expands its moral dimension to the care of creation.

CULTURE, EDUCATION, AND GOD

Laudato Si' includes calls for education with respect to concern for the environment. Nonetheless, these exhortations are especially subject to misunderstanding as they may fall prey to the reductionist tendency to focus only on externals such as recycling and pollution. The mode of education must not only address issues of concern for the natural environment, but also must seek to foster an alternative to the dominance of the technocratic paradigm and its accompanying relativism as well as the twin danger of cancelling out the difference between human beings and all other creatures. Education in environmental care thus needs to begin with a recovery of the distinctive role of human beings within creation, the recognition of God as the Creator, as well as on the need to guide and form the passions and reason of individuals. *Laudato Si'* calls for an education that is irreducibly moral in character.

Laudato Si''s emphasis on moral education becomes clearer when placed in the context of another theme from C. S. Lewis's *The Abolition of Man*. The casual reader may well be surprised to find that Lewis's philosophical essay is subtitled "Or Reflections on Education with Special Reference to the Teaching of English in the Upper Forms of Schools." The central focus on education may be explained in two ways. First, and most simply, Lewis himself taught at Oxford for most of his professional life and then finally held an academic chair at Cambridge. Thus, he was especially attuned to the experience of teaching literature to university students and to the philosophical implications inescapably involved. Second, *The Abolition of Man* stands unique among anti-relativist essays insofar as it is not a direct argument against relativism. Instead, it is an argument that the cultures of the West in general and of England in particular have been engaged in a false approach to education, one that undermines the existence of moral truths. The argument for objective moral value is not so much a philosophical argument as an observation of what traditional cultures have sought to do through education and then to contrast such an education to a dominant strand of modern education that inculcates moral relativism and skepticism. Gilbert Meilaender summarizes Lewis's stance on education as follows: "We can see, then, that life within the structure of the Tao [the recognition of objective moral value] is, for Lewis, a way of wisdom rather than a way of power. It is the task of moral education to set limits to what we will do in search of the rainbow's end—to set limits, lest that desire should lead to the abolition of man."[59]

As with Lewis, the Pope understands that these philosophical and theological issues come to the fore in education and in the formation of the culture: "There needs to be a distinctive way of looking at things, a way of thinking, policies, an educational programme, a lifestyle and a spirituality which together generate resistance to the assault of the technocratic paradigm."[60] There must be resistance to exploitation fostered through the virtues of cultivation and care: "It cannot be maintained that empirical science provides a complete explanation of life, the interplay of all creatures and the whole of reality. This would be to breach the limits imposed by its own methodology."[61] Caring for both human creatures and sub-human creation reinforces the proper worth of each.

To care for creation properly requires that we recognize the beginning and end of creation in God. Two distinctions thus are necessary: the distinction between human beings and sub-human creation, and the more fundamental distinction between creation and God. As Pope Francis succinctly states, "We are not God."[62] This utterance counters a false divinization of human beings that grants them unlimited power: "The best way to restore men and women to their rightful place, putting an end to their claim to absolute dominion over the earth, is to speak once more of the figure of a Father who creates and who alone owns the world. Otherwise, human beings will always try to impose their own laws and interests on reality."[63] The recognition of God as Creator shows that there are givens to reality to which human beings are called to conform. It is our home, yes, but it is ultimately God's creation.

Humans are not easily regulated animals, but creatures with monstrous appetites and desires so large that they could easily consume themselves, let alone the planet. Pope Francis calls for sobriety to temper excessive consumption, for obedience to temper autonomy, and for theism to temper subjectivism: "It is not easy to promote this kind of healthy humility or happy sobriety when we consider ourselves autonomous, when we exclude God from our lives or replace him with our own ego, and think that our subjective feelings can define what is right and what is wrong."[64] A strong sense of God and of right and wrong drive the duty to care for those in most need of our assistance, not only the lower creatures surrounding us, but especially the poor among our fellow humans. The encyclical thus places at the forefront of environmental concern two great truths that are so counter-cultural in the present moment: the protological, the uniqueness of God as Creator, and the anthropological, the uniqueness of humans as rational and free.

When the modern environmental movement continues to exclude God and morality, it inadvertently, but inevitably, weakens itself to confront the very forces that lead to degradation of the environment. Consider another insight from Lewis' *Abolition of Man*: "In a sort of ghastly simplicity we remove the organ and demand the function. We make men without chests and expect of them virtue and enterprise. We laugh at honour and are shocked to find traitors in our midst. We castrate and bid the geldings be fruitful."[65] Consider how often education at contemporary universities critiques traditional sexual morality as repressive or unjustly restraining self-expression and yet simultaneously expects restraint in the use of natural resources. As an alternative, Pope Francis connects the love of creation to the renunciation of desires: "the poverty and austerity of Saint Francis were no mere veneer of asceticism, but something much more radical: a refusal to turn reality into an object simply to be used and controlled."[66]

It is the human person who must guide the almighty will in both social relations and relations with the rest of creation. A similar connection was made early in *Laudato Si'*: "Pope Benedict asked us to recognize that the natural environment has been gravely damaged by our irresponsible behaviour. The social environment has also suffered damage. Both are ultimately due to the same evil: the notion that there are no indisputable truths to guide our lives, and hence human freedom is limitless."[67] The evil highlighted here is the failure to recognize properly the moral dimension of the human person as expressed in traditional morality and the natural law. Pope Francis reveals the harsh realism of a surgeon when he takes stock of the present state of societies: "When the culture itself is corrupt and objective truth and universally valid principles are no longer upheld, then laws can only be seen as arbitrary impositions or obstacles to be avoided."[68] Environmental policies are not sufficient; there are no shortcuts to the renewal of the culture of caring.

CONCLUSION: A NEW ENVIRONMENTALISM OF CARE

Catholic intellectual life was enriched by Pope Saint John Paul II's ability to discern the truths and the errors within contemporary intellectual and societal movements. He confronted the false humanism of Marxism with a renewed Christian humanism seeing the person as fully revealed in the mystery of the Word incarnate. [69] John Paul II likewise called for a new feminism distinguished by a recovery of the "genius" particularly feminine.[70] In these instances, there was a significant departure from the standard humanism and feminism that characterized the twentieth century.

Pope Francis has issued another "significant departure" from the standard environmentalism of recent decades in *Laudato Si'*. The encyclical reframes the environmental movement as a response to the dominance of a technological paradigm that first and foremost fails to recognize the distinctively human, the moral level of human existence, and the necessarily theological dimension of human life. As a shock to many contemporary readers, the encyclical depicts the enemy of care for the environment as moral relativism. The

Pope situates recycling, pollution, and species preservation into a necessary recovery of moral truths—and theological truths. This concern for the reduction of the human person to his material parts for manipulation was presciently highlighted in C. S. Lewis's *The Abolition of Man* in the early 1940s. The revelations about the sale of fetal human body parts that surfaced in 2015 show that contemporary societies in the West are indeed failing to care for our common home. *Laudato Si'* calls for a new environmentalism rooted in the recognition of the objective moral order and the resulting care for creation by human beings made in the image and likeness of God—a natural law ethic of care. The care for the environment cannot progress without a recognition of moral truths since care is itself a moral activity.

NOTES

1. Here are two news articles with those attributed titles: "Pope's Climate Change Encyclical Tells Rich Nations: Pay Your Debt to the Poor," *The Guardian*, 18 June 2015, (www.guardian.com, accessed 1 August 2016); and "Pope Francis' Encyclical on the Environment," *America*, 11 June 2015 (www.americamagazine.org, accessed 1 August 2016).
2. See www.oed.com (accessed 1 August 2016).
3. Various translations of this encyclical's subtitle cover the same basic meaning as the English word "care": for example, in French "*suavegarde*," in Spanish "*cuidado*," in Italian "*cura*," in German "*sorge*," in Latin, "*colenda*," as published at www.vatican.va (accessed 1 August 2016).
4. *Summa Theologiae* II-II, q.23. a. 1; 2 Peter 1:4 Revised Standard Version Catholic Edition (RSVCE).
5. 1 Peter 5:7, RSVCE.
6. Pope Francis, Encyclical Letter *Laudato Si'*, 24 May 2015, hereafter cited as *LS*. Pope Francis introduces this theme of interconnectedness in the context of the opening chapters of Genesis and the mystery of creation and fall: "These ancient stories, full of symbolism, bear witness to a conviction which we today share, that everything is interconnected, and that genuine care for our own lives and our relationships with nature is inseparable from fraternity, justice and faithfulness to others" (*LS* no. 70). He later expands this theme with a Trinitarian dimension: "The human person grows more, matures more and is sanctified more to the extent that he or she enters into relationships, going out from themselves to live in communion with God, with others and with all creatures. ... Everything is interconnected, and this invites us to develop a spirituality of that global solidarity which flows from the mystery of the Trinity" (*LS* no. 240).

7. *LS* no. 11, italics added. Hereafter all italicization of "care" from *LS* is added unless otherwise noted.
8. *LS* no. 14.
9. *LS* no. 64.
10. *LS* no. 79.
11. *LS* no. 6, citing Pope Benedict XVI, Encyclical Letter *Caritas in Veritate* (29 June 2009), 51: AAS 101 (2009), 687.
12. *LS* no. 119.
13. *LS* no. 139.
14. *LS* no. 141.
15. *LS* no. 162.
16. *LS* no. 10.
17. *LS* no. 228. For an insightful Aristotelian and Thomistic analysis of ordered interconnections among the various natures of things within creation and of the Creator, see Charles Morerod, OP, "A World of Natures and the Presence of God," *Nova et Vetera*, English Edition, Vol. 10, No. 1 (2012): 215-31.
18. *LS* no. 231.
19. *LS* no. 208.
20. *LS* no. 241.
21. *LS* no. 242.
22. *LS* no. 242.
23. *LS* no. 167.
24. *LS* no. 118.
25. *LS* no. 106.
26. *LS* no. 119.
27. *LS* no. 224.
28. *LS* no. 107.
29. For a sustained analysis of the order present in creation and the relationship to stewardship, see Stephen Hipp, "Nature's Finality and the Stewardship of Creation According to Saint Thomas Aquinas," *Nova et Vetera*, English Edition, Vol. 10, No. 1 (2012), 143-91.
30. *LS* no. 117.
31. *LS* no. 136. Then Cardinal Joseph Ratzinger explicitly links the themes of the objectification of the human person and embryonic harvesting in the 2004 preface to his *Introduction to Christianity*: "Man is becoming a technological object while vanishing to an ever greater degree as a human subject, and he has only himself to blame. When human embryos are artificially 'cultivated' so as to have 'research material' and to obtain a supply of organs, which then are supposed to benefit other human begins, there is scarcely an outcry, because so few are horrified any more" (San Francisco: Ignatius Press, 2004), 17.
32. See *LS* no. 117. This is why the language of the encyclical is not anti-doctrinal, even when it emphasizes that doctrines must be fully embraced by the

person in a way of life: "More than in ideas or concepts as such, I am interested in how such a spirituality can motivate us to a more passionate concern for the protection of our world. A commitment this lofty cannot be sustained by doctrine alone, without a spirituality capable of inspiring us, without an 'interior impulse which encourages, motivates, nourishes and gives meaning to our individual and communal activity,'" no. 216, citing Apostolic Exhortation *Evangelii Gaudium* (24 Nov 2013), 261: AAS 105 (2013), 1124).

33. *LS* no. 81.
34. *LS* no. 78.
35. *LS* no. 155.
36. Abortion and exploitation of the unborn are condemned in the following places in *Laudato Si'*: nos. 117, 120, 136.
37. *LS* no. 162.
38. *LS* cites PP only once in no. 127: "We need to remember that men and women have 'the capacity to improve their lot, to further their moral growth and to develop their spiritual endowments,'" citing Paul VI, Encyclical Letter *Populorum Progressio* (26 March 1967), 34: AAS 59 (1967), 274. Interestingly, this is the same section that develops the critique of technocracy.
39. *PP*, no. 34.
40. *PP* no. 34. The alternative to the technocratic paradigm is a view of human nature that acknowledges its moral and spiritual dimensions and the moral and spiritual truths within these dimensions. See no. 34: "Organized programs designed to increase productivity should have but one aim: *to serve human nature*. They should reduce inequities, eliminate discrimination, free men from the bonds of servitude, and thus give them the capacity, in the sphere of temporal realities, to improve their lot, to further their moral growth and to develop their spiritual endowments. When we speak of development, we should mean social progress as well as economic growth" (italics added).
41. C. S. Lewis, *The Abolition of Man: Or Reflections on Education with Special Reference to the Teaching of English in the Upper Forms of Schools* (New York: Touchstone, Simon & Schuster, 1996, originally published 1944), 73.
42. In 1988, then Cardinal Joseph Ratzinger gave an address entitled "Consumer Materialism and Christian Hope" at Cambridge University, where C. S. Lewis held an academic chair, and in fact drew upon Lewis' *The Abolition of Man*, linking specifically the loss of the natural moral law and the resulting lack of limits on what humans may do to each other and to the world: "This reduction of nature to demonstrable and thus pliable facts has consequences: no moral message outside of ourselves can reach us anymore. ... Lewis raised this warning during the Second World War because he saw how, with the destruction of morality, the very capacity to defend his nation against the onslaught of barbarism was imperiled. ... This seems to me to be a comment of great import: the opposing worldviews of today, have a common

starting point in the rejection of the natural moral law and the reduction of the world to 'mere' acts. ... The 'abolition of man' which follows from making absolute one method of coming to knowledge is the clear distortion of this worldview as well." (Text available at http://catholicexchange.com/framing-benedict, accessed 1 August 2016.) This public lecture at Cambridge was further developed in a published article that can be found in *A Turning Point for Europe?* (San Francisco, CA: Ignatius Press, 2010).
43. *The Abolition of Man*, 35.
44. Ibid., 77.
45. Ibid., 80.
46. *LS* no. 123.
47. *LS* no. 123.
48. *LS* no. 10.
49. *LS* no. 119.
50. See *LS* no. 155 for "moral law"; no. 115 for "moral structure."
51. *Summa Theologiae*, I-II, q. 94, a. 2: "since every agent acts for an end under the aspect of good (rationem boni)."
52. *ST*, I-II, q. 94, a. 2. Note that precepts follow from inclinations: "According to the order of natural inclinations, is the order of the precepts of the natural law."
53. *ST*, I-II, q. 94, a. 2.
54. *ST* I, q. 1, a. 1: "Even as regards those truths about God which human reason could have discovered, it was necessary that man should be taught by a divine revelation; because the truth about God such as reason could discover, would only be known by a few, and that after a long time, and with the admixture of many errors." For a fuller discussion of the role of the knowledge of God and the natural law see Fulvio Di Blasi, *God and the Natural Law: A Rereading of Thomas Aquinas* (South Bend, IN: St. Augustine's, 2006); Oscar J. Brown, *Natural Rectitude and Divine Law in Aquinas* (Toronto: Pontifical Institute of Mediaeval Studies, 1981), 37-52; Romanus Cessario, O.P., *Introduction to Moral Theology* (Washington, DC: Catholic University of America Press, 2001), 77-84; Yves R. Simon, *The Tradition of Natural Law: A Philosopher's Reflections*, edited by Vukan Kuic (New York: Fordham University Press, 1992), 62-66.
55. *LS* no. 155.
56. *LS* no. 115: "When human beings fail to find their true place in this world, they misunderstand themselves and end up acting against themselves: 'Not only has God given the earth to man, who must use it with respect for the original good purpose for which it was given, but, man too is God's gift to man. He must therefore respect the natural and moral structure with which he has been endowed,'" citing John Paul II, Encyclical Letter *Centesimus Annus* (1 May 1991), 38: AAS 83 (1991), 841 [93].
57. *LS* no. 11.

58. *LS* no. 155, citing the Address to the German Bundestag, Berlin (22 September 2011): AAS 103 (2011), 668. Note that the Bundestag is the national parliament of the Federal Republic of Germany.
59. "On Moral Knowledge," in *The Cambridge Companion to C. S. Lewis*, edited by Robert MacSwain and Michael Ward (New York: Cambridge University Press, 2010), 119-131, 130.
60. *LS* no. 111.
61. *LS* no. 199.
62. *LS* no. 67. This same paragraph ends with an exegesis of Gen. 2:15 and the exhortation to "till and keep" the garden now explained through the ethic of care: "'keeping' means caring, protecting, overseeing and preserving." See also LS no. 6 quoting Benedict XVI.
63. *LS* no. 75.
64. *LS* no. 224.
65. *The Abolition of Man*, 37.
66. *LS* no. 11.
67. *LS* no. 11.
68. *LS* no. 123.
69. See for example in his citing of *Gaudium et Spes* no. 22 in his encyclical, *Redepmtor Hominis* no. 8, 4 March 1979; see also George Weigel, *Witness to Hope: The Biography of Pope John Paul II* (New York: Harper Collins, 1999).
70. Pope John Paul II, Apostolic Letter, *Mulieris Dignitatem* no. 30, 15 August 1988.

NATURAL LAW AND THE IMITATION OF NATURE: A THOMISTIC DEVELOPMENT OF HUMAN ECOLOGY

Scott Jude Roniger

> "Learn from the way the wild flowers grow."
> –Jesus of Nazareth

> "The river is a strong brown god."
> –T.S. Eliot

Meditating on the example of St. Francis of Assisi, Pope Francis says, "If we approach nature and the environment without this openness to awe and wonder, if we no longer speak the language of fraternity and beauty in our relationship with the world, our attitude will be that of masters, consumers, ruthless exploiters, unable to set limits on their immediate needs. By contrast, if we feel intimately united with all that exists, then sobriety and care will well up spontaneously."[1] At numerous points in the encyclical, he says that the natural world carries a message, an intelligibility, pointing toward the Creator of the cosmos, and that we must learn to rediscover this "message contained in the structure of nature itself."[2] Further, the Pontiff says that an authentic human ecology must heed these messages embedded within the natural environment, which speak to us of God, show the intimate interconnectedness of all reality, and manifest the world of nature as worthy of respect.

In this article, I will develop these ideas by turning to Thomas Aquinas's understanding of the human person's "imitation of nature" and its connection to his theory of natural law. I will suggest that Aquinas's theory can complement and extend the pedagogical role assigned to the natural world by Pope Francis. While Pope Francis shows how the natural world, as distinct from human persons and their social and political lives, can "teach" the thoughtful observer about the goodness of God who creates and sustains the cosmos, Aquinas presents the world of nature as educative of the human intellect in various senses. For Aquinas, the world of nature not only speaks of its Creator, but it also forms the very structure of our moral thinking such that our understanding of what is morally good and hence our discovery of the natural law is bound up with our grasp of the manner in which entities in the natural world operate and interact. Thus, our "openness to awe and wonder" at the natural world is at the root of our moral lives since, according to Aquinas, the world of non-human nature has a morally pedagogical role for human agents.

HOW DO WE RELATE TO THE NATURAL WORLD? THREE RESPONSES

As is well-known, René Descartes set the trajectory for modern thought and for the characteristically modern approach to the relationship between human beings and the natural world. Descartes, in what Allan Bloom calls "that famous fund-raising brochure,"[3] promises new freedoms and possibilities for humanity through the development of medicine and technology. Descartes says that we should replace that "speculative philosophy taught in the schools" and find instead a new practical philosophy, "by means of which, knowing the force and actions of fire, water, air, the stars, the heavens, and all the other bodies that surround us, just as distinctly as we know the various skills of our craftsmen, we might be able, in the same way, to use them for all the purposes for which they are appropriate and thus render ourselves, as it were, masters and possessors of nature."[4] To accomplish his project of rendering human beings masters and possessors of nature, Descartes develops his philosophical system by claiming that the classic doctrine of substantial forms is simply unnecessary, and he proceeds to eviscerate the notion of final causality that is so crucial to classical Aristotelian philosophy.[5]

Descartes rejects the notion of final causality at least in part because he claimed that he was not so presumptuous as to think he could understand the mind of God. Descartes says:

> Since I know that my nature is very weak and limited, whereas the nature of God is immense, incomprehensible, and infinite, this is sufficient for me also to know that he can make innumerable things whose causes escape me. For this reason alone the entire class of causes which people customarily derive from a thing's "end," I judge to be utterly useless in physics. It is not without rashness that I think myself capable of inquiring into the ends of God.[6]

Thus, Descartes initiates what Denise Des Chene calls "a world without ends."[7] By "end," I mean the *telos* or perfected state of an entity, the excellence of that entity according to its kind; the end of a thing being that for the sake of which it naturally undertakes its characteristic movements. Robert Sokolowski says, "[Ends] come about concomitantly with the things they belong to. Things might spring into being when they are generated or made or occur by accident, but ends do not arise without the thing. An end is the finished, perfected state of a thing, the thing when it is acting well as what it is."[8] Regarding Descartes's vision of a world without ends, Des Chene asks "What becomes of finality in the new world of *res extensae*? The brief answer is: nothing…Not just final causes, but the directedness essential to the Aristotelian concept of change, are absent."[9] According to Des Chene, the loss of finality, which Robert Sokolowski calls "the deletion of the ends of things,"[10] is inextricably tied to the quantitative understanding of the natural world. Des Chene says, "To hold that the nature of corporeal substance is constituted by extension is to deny that corporeal substance could have active powers."[11] The neglect of substantial form and the concomitant reduction of natural things to *res exstensae* result in the elimination of final causality, or the "deletion of the ends of things." With Descartes, we can manipulate the corporal world through the mathematical study of entities considered only as extended things, which leads to an almost exclusive reliance on efficient causality in our understanding of entities and their characteristic movements. We can profitably ask: How does this conception of the natural world affect our morality? Des Chene says, "The only morality, it would seem, to be gleaned from the natural world so understood consists in the unique admonition: do what you will."[12]

After Descartes, John Locke works out some of the logic of living in a world without ends. In the *Second Treatise of Government*, Locke says, "God, who hath given the world to men in common, hath also given them reason to make use of it to the best advantage of life, and convenience."[13] Although the earth is common to all men, the labor of a person's body and the work of his hands are properly his,[14] and "it is *labour* indeed that *puts the difference of value* on every thing."[15] Locke says that the land, the world of non-human nature, is simply a waste: "Land that is left wholly to nature, that hath no improvement of pasture . . . is called, as indeed it is, *waste*; and we shall find the benefit of it amount to little more than nothing."[16] Thus, God gives us the land in common, but He has given us nothing more than a wasteland that has no benefit for human agents apart from the labor that we invest into it.

Descartes and Locke can be taken to represent the modern understanding of the relationship between human agents and the natural world. From this viewpoint, human agents are masters and possessors of a natural world that is, prior to the intervention of human labor and technology, nothing more than a wasteland.

The recent movement known as "post-humanism" stands at the opposite extreme from the position developed in the earlier modern period by Descartes and Locke. Jedediah Purdy says that "post-humanism," at least in some of its more radical forms, calls for the "leveling [of] the hierarchical divide between human and nonhuman by blurring that boundary."[17] According to this view, "we should not think of the natural world as inert matter moved by mute physical laws, but as acting upon us."[18] Purdy says that post-humanist thinkers claim that "we are less distinct from the rest of nature than we often imagine,"[19] and therefore post-humanists "tend to assert that all forms of life have equal value in principle."[20] The post-humanists attempt to point to the similarities between all forms of organic life in order to "nudge humans away from their special place at the center of the world,"[21] and although Purdy himself does not agree on all points with the post-humanists, he encourages us to take their "strange intuitions" seriously. While modernity as exemplified by Descartes and Locke degrades the inherent excellences of the natural world and exaggerates our role in shaping it, the post-humanists degrade human beings in their attempt to exalt the world of nature.

Thomistic natural law theory and the doctrine of the imitation of nature offer us a middle path between these two extremes. For Aquinas and the subsequent Thomistic tradition, the natural law governs us (1) according to our nature as intelligent, free, and responsible agents and (2) according to the natures of things that we experience in the natural world. Thus, Thomistic natural law understands the obligations that are imposed upon us by nature in reference to our end (telos), to what we ought to be according to what we are as human beings, and these obligations arise in conjunction with our experience of the natural ends of things in the world.

THREE FOCI OF ORDER

In *Laudato Si'*, Pope Francis speaks of the need for human ecology to unite three principal aspects: faith in God as loving Creator, concern for and responsible stewardship of the environment, and love for our fellow human beings. He says, "Everything is related, and we human beings are united as brothers and sisters on a wonderful pilgrimage, woven together by the love God has for each of His creatures and which also unites us in fond affection with brother sun, sister moon, brother river, and mother earth."[22] Therefore, the issue of building an integral human ecology forces us to confront the distinctions and relationships between (1) God, (2) the natural world, and (3) human beings made in the *imago Dei*.

How can Thomistic natural law theory assist us in this endeavor? To answer this question, we can turn to Yves Simon's work on the natural law. Simon says that there is an "eternal return" of natural law thinking despite the vast changes that have taken place between pre-modern and modern philosophies, social institutions, and political forms.[23] Part of the reason for this "eternal return" of the natural law is the fact that a natural law theory, as Simon says, seeks to discover the "prior premises" of human positive law.[24] The natural law premises are "prior" in a primarily ontological sense; the "prior" is not just chronological in the sense that we have these issues even before explicitly engaging in politics, but also permanent and ontological, in that they are the constant source of positive law and also the basis for our ethical interaction. Thus, natural law seeks to answer ultimate questions about the source of authority and justice and to clarify the sources of moral interaction. For Aquinas (and Simon), "prior" to the order in human affairs introduced by the positive law and political reforms, human life and the natural world already exhibit an ordered structure. Therefore, an investigation into natural law as the "prior premises" for positive law and for moral interaction involves the distinction between "three foci of order" that are more ontologically fundamental than the positive law.

Building upon Simon's thought, Russell Hittinger says that the prior premises of natural law coalesce around the three foci of "order in nature, order in the human mind, and order in the divine mind."[25] In response to the question "What is a theory of natural law a theory of?" Hittinger says:

> In the first place, natural law can be regarded as an issue of propositions that are first in the order of practical cognition. On this view, a philosophical account of natural law endeavors to bring into focus those "reasons for action" antecedent to reasons yielded through practical deliberation and judgment. In the second place, natural law can also be regarded as an issue of nature or human nature, in which case natural law is not only a problem of the logic and epistemology of practical reason, but also a problem of how practical reason is situated in a broader order of causality. Finally, natural law can be approached not only as order in the mind or in nature, but as the ordinance of a divine lawgiver.[26]

These three foci provide both a foundation and a framework for the institution of positive law in a political community.

We identify (1) order "in" the human mind in the form of propositions that provide direction for moral action prior to our individual deliberations and decisions about what must be done in a concrete situation. These general propositions, such as the precepts to seek good and avoid evil, to seek family and social life, and to pursue the truth about God, as well as the prohibitions against murder or adultery, provide a basis for moral deliberation and judgment. However, order in the human mind must be seen in relation to (2) a broader order of causality within the natural world. "Order in nature" refers to the realm of entities having their own inner principles of motion and rest as distinct from the world of human production; it is the world of *physis* in distinction from *technê*. Aristotle says:

> Of things that exist, some exist by nature, some from other causes. By nature the animals and their parts exist, and the plants and the simple bodies . . . for we say that these and the like exist by nature. All the things mentioned plainly differ from things which are not constituted by nature. For each of them has within itself a principle of motion and of stationariness (in respect of place, or of growth and decrease, or by way of alteration). On the other hand, a bed and a coat and anything else of that sort, qua receiving these designations – i.e. in so far as they are products of art – have no innate impulse to change.[27]

As we will discuss in more detail, the order in the human mind is shaped by our interactions with the natural entities that we, in company with others, confront in experience. Finally, these first two foci of order are both seen as expressions of (3) order "in" the divine mind. Natural law thinking can provide a foundation for human ecology by distinguishing these three foci of order and describing how they are integrated with each other.

For Aquinas, order in the human mind and order in nature are not laws in themselves. Rather, they are law-abiding or expressions of law. Aquinas is a pre-modern thinker, and his conception of the natural law is importantly distinct from both Locke, who says that natural law is human reason,[28] and Jean-Jacques Rousseau, who says that natural law is the voice of nature (*la voix de la nature*).[29] While Locke locates natural law exclusively in the order of the human mind and Rousseau reduces natural law to the order in nature,

Aquinas says order in the divine mind is the source of the natural law.[30] This claim raises a crucial question concerning how order in the human mind and order in nature depend upon order in the divine mind, and Aquinas's doctrine of the human agent's imitation of nature can help us formulate an answer.

AQUINAS AND THE IMITATION OF NATURE

For Aquinas, there are at least two ways in which the order of nature is a source of instruction for human agents.[31] In both speculative and practical thought, the order in nature has a central role in forming the human intellect. First, in the speculative realm Aquinas says that the order manifest in the operations and interconnections of entities in the natural world point to the existence of God. Not only is this order in nature the basis of the fifth way of proving God's existence, but Aquinas also mentions a "pre-philosophical" grasp of the existence of God based on our encounter with the order of the natural world. He says, "Man can immediately reach some sort of knowledge of God by natural reason. For, when men see that things in nature run according to a definite order, and that ordering does not occur without an orderer, they perceive in most cases that there is some orderer of the things that we see. But who or what kind of being, or whether there is but one orderer of nature, is not yet grasped immediately in this general consideration."[32] This nascent and often confused knowledge of God is not innate, nor is it the fruit of polished metaphysical argument, but nevertheless Aquinas sees the order in the natural world as educating the human agent about the existence of God. Through our experience of nature, we can behold some truth, albeit nebulous, about the existence of God understood as the source of cosmic order.

More importantly for our purposes, Aquinas says that the order of human actions is also taken from the order that we originally behold in the natural world. Thus, not only speculative thinking, but also our practical intellect is formed by our encounter with nature. He says, "The principles of reason are those things that are according to nature; for reason, having presupposed the things that are determined by nature, disposes other things in a concordant way. And this is apparent both in the speculative and in the practical order."[33] According to Aquinas, "Human acts can be regulated according to the rule of human reason, which is gleaned (*sumitur*) from the created things that man naturally knows."[34] For Aquinas, the practical life of human agents consists in ordering our speech, actions, and emotions in view of common goods, and it is the job of the ethicist to study the practical order that we must introduce into our lives.[35] However, how is the rule of human reason "gleaned from the created things that man naturally knows"?

In the *Physics*, Aristotle says that art, understood broadly as the realm of skilled human production, imitates nature.[36] Commenting on this text, Aquinas says,

> The reason for saying that art imitates nature (*ars imitatur naturam*) is the following. Knowledge is the principle of operation in art and all of our knowledge is gathered through the senses from sensible and natural things. Therefore, in works of art (*in artificialibus*) we operate similarly to natural things. And so, natural things are imitable by art, because all nature is ordered to its end (*tota natura ordinatur ad finem suum*) by some intellective principle, and thus the work of nature seems to be the work of intelligence, as it proceeds to certain ends through determinate means. This is what art imitates in its operation.[37]

In this passage, Aquinas says that the works of nature manifest themselves to us as works of intelligence precisely insofar as natural entities are ordered to their proper ends. The telic, end-directed motions of natural things reveal an order in the natural world, and it is precisely this ordered movement to natural ends that reason beholds in the world and imitates in its own actions. Human agents will realize this order according to their own nature, that is, we will achieve our end according to the mode of intelligence and free choice, but natural entities provide us with an example of how agents act for and achieve ends. Thus, we can see a natural entity's movement to its fitting end as a source of intelligibility in the natural world that serves to educate the human mind about its own actions.

However, it is not simply that human reason beholds individual entities acting in an ordered way toward their own specific ends. According to both Aristotle and Aquinas, a natural agent's movement toward its end propels it into an integrated lattice of interacting natures. That is, the natural entity's order to its perfection is always ingrained in a more expansive order of all the "parts" of the natural world to each other. Aristotle says, "And all things are ordered together somehow, but not all alike, both fishes and fowls and plants; and the world is not such that one thing has nothing to do with another, but they are connected. For all are ordered together to one end."[38] Thus, each individual thing is inclined toward its perfection by operating within a wider web of interacting natures.

We can therefore distinguish between two kinds, or two levels, of order in nature: (1) the order of each entity toward its perfection (the order of the part to its perfection within the whole), and (2) the order of all natural things mutually influencing each other and their environment (the order of the whole itself, or the order of all the natures to each other within the whole). Jacques Maritain captured the relation of these two levels of order with the phrase "The Republic of Natures."[39] The key is to understand that these kinds of order are not merely unopposed, but rather they are dependent upon each other and complementary; the interaction of different natures on the larger scale is organized harmoniously precisely through each individual nature operating according to its inherent dynamism for its perfection.[40]

Aquinas says that the human agent's imitation of nature includes both of these levels of order. Aquinas says:

> Now nature in its operation proceeds from the simple to the complex, so that in the things that come about through the operation of nature, that which is most complex is perfect and whole and constitutes the end of the other things, as is apparent in the case of every whole with respect to its parts. Hence human reason also, operating from the simple to the complex, proceeds as it were from the imperfect to the perfect. [41]

In this text, we see that human agents imitate nature by arranging parts in view of a whole. This structure of human thinking is at the root of political life and the notion of the common good; we can only intelligently undertake common action for common ends if we understand how simple elements must be ordered to complex wholes. Aquinas applies the above principle to political life:

> Now since human reason has to order not only the things that are used by man but also men themselves, who are ruled by reason, it proceeds in both cases from the simple to the complex. For example, in the case of the things used by man, he builds a ship out of wood and a house out of wood and stones. In the case of men themselves, for example, it orders many men into some one community. Of which communities, since there are diverse grades and orders, the ultimate is the community of the city ordered to the essential completeness of human life. Hence, among all human communities it (the city) is most perfect.[42]

Both nature and reason order simple and imperfect things to complex and perfect ones. In the case of human reason, we dispose not only the things that we must use, such as wood for ships, but we also order human beings themselves into more complex social and political communities. Therefore, for Aquinas the imitation of nature plays a crucial role in the very genesis of political life.

Further, just as with "parts" of more complex wholes within the natural world, the person considered as a "part" of a given community finds his perfection within the whole of a given social and political body. For example, in a school community, the leaders will have to see how each teacher and each class fit as "parts" ordered to the common end of educating students, and the teacher considered as a part of the community must understand that his perfection comes by contributing to the good of the whole school. Most importantly, an individual person can find happiness only as a virtuous member of a family, while the family itself is more perfect as a family when it exists within a well-ordered social and political structure. Thus, the imitation of nature for Aquinas refers to the grasp of formal structures of the natural world (especially the ordering of parts to wholes) that serve as models for general principles of practical thought.[43]

Aquinas's conception of the imitation of nature does not imply that the establishment of orderly political regimes is somehow automatic. Clearly, human agents must learn how best to organize any given whole of which they are a part in view of the common good as an end, but Aquinas's point is that the formal structure of the simple part(s) in relation to the complex whole is first understood or discovered in our encounter with the natural world. Because the natural world exhibits this part-to-whole structure, we learn from it and imitate it by ordering our own lives and associations accordingly. Thus, Aquinas's doctrine of the imitation of nature can be understood as a description of the fundamental structures of human practical thought that enable human agents naturally to pursue political life. The human person, just as every other natural being, is ordered to his perfection through characteristic movements and operations that introduce him into more complex interactions with other people and with the world itself. In the *De regno*, Aquinas says:

> The light of reason is placed by nature in every man, to guide him in his acts towards his end. Wherefore, if man were intended to live alone, as many animals do, he would require no other guide to his end. Each man would be a king unto himself, under God, the highest King, inasmuch as he would direct himself in his acts by the light of reason given him from on high. Yet it is natural for man, more than for any other animal, to be a social and political animal, to live in a group.[44]

While we have to learn how to construct just social and political associations, we do not have to be taught to pursue social and political life. The establishment of just political regimes is an achievement of human intelligence and virtue and thus has the human intellect as its principle cause, but the natural inclination to political and social life, or the seeds of which the finished city is the fruit, exists in man by nature. The doctrine of the imitation of nature shows us the characteristic modes of operation of human reason that make our pursuit of political life possible. For Aquinas, the human mind is ordered naturally to its end of social and political life precisely by imitating the order it witnesses in the natural world.

We have now seen that the natural world (1) speaks of its creator and (2) offers a model of order that the human intellect naturally apprehends and imitates. How can these two aspects be united? In the prologue to his commentary on Aristotle's *Politics*, Aquinas says:

> As the Philosopher teaches in *Physics II*, art imitates nature. The reason for this is that, as principles stand relative to each other, so also proportionately stand their operations and effects. Now, the principle of those things that are brought about by art is the human intellect, which in virtue of some measure of likeness is derived from the divine intellect, which is the principle of natural things. Hence it is necessary that the operations of art also imitate the operations of nature; and those things that are by virtue of art imitate those things that are in nature. For, if someone who is an instructor in some art were to bring about a work of the art, it would be necessary that the disciple who received the art from him look to that teacher's work so as himself to work in imitation of that. And therefore the human intellect, to which intelligible light is derived from the divine intellect, necessarily has it that in those things which it makes it be informed from inspection of those things which have been made naturally so as to operate similarly.[45]

Here, Aquinas likens the human agent encountering the natural world to a pupil standing in front of the masterpiece of his teacher. For the student to become an excellent artist, he has to learn from and imitate the skill of composition, the ordering of parts to the whole that he witnesses in the masterpiece of his teacher. In an analogous way, human agents must imitate the ordering of things to their end and of parts to their whole that we discover in the natural world.[46]

But we can ask, what exactly is the student imitating when he begins his own work? In one sense, he is imitating the work of art that he has studied, but more importantly he is imitating his teacher. That is, he is learning from and imitating his teacher precisely by imitating his teacher's work of art. Aquinas is saying that human agents imitate the divine wisdom, which is the source both of the natural world and the human intellect, precisely by learning from and imitating the natural world. Because the natural world is in fact the expression of God's wisdom, we imitate the divine artist by imitating the natural world.

At this point, one may object that Aquinas's use of the principle that art and reason imitate nature depends upon first seeing God as the principle both of human reason and the world of nature. In short, it requires seeing nature as a manifestation of divine wisdom. However, Aquinas's texts on the imitation of nature should be read in a more nuanced way. Aquinas often presents his thought according to what is first in the order of being as distinct from what is first in the order of discovery; that is, he speaks from the vantage point of wisdom and thus views things from God to nature. In the text just quoted, in which Aquinas says that the human person imitates nature as the handiwork of God, he is presenting his work according to what is first in being (and hence last in discovery). Although Thomas thinks that we should (and in fact do) quickly relate the order apparent in nature to something like a god, philosophically the consideration of the divine comes as a conclusion, not a starting point. Lawrence Dewan says, "Reason puts nature first, not precisely because nature reveals its divine origin, but because reason sees ontological priority. Goodness is seen in ontological order, and reason's giving nature priority is the recognition of that order. The ontologically determinate (i.e., nature) has more of the aspect of being than has the ontologically determinable (the operable or choosable)."[47] Thus, in the order of discovery, our encounter with the natural world comes first, and it is here, in the philosophical order of discovery, that Aquinas presents the natural world as having a double function in relation to the human mind: in Dewan's terms, the ontologically determinate (nature) functions both (1) as a springboard to knowledge of the divine ordering mind and (2) as a model for the ontologically determinable (art and human action).

Aquinas goes on to apply this doctrine of reason imitating nature in numerous places in the *secunda secundae*. He argues that just as there is a hierarchy of natural things, so too there should be a corresponding hierarchy in human associations, with subordinate members properly disposed to obey their superiors.[48] Aquinas even argues that virtue imitates nature because it pertains to virtue to show love and give benefits to the people in our lives according to a certain order. Although there are extreme cases, generally speaking we should assist members of our family, then members of our local community, and then members of our wider political community, and Aquinas says this virtuous ordering of human relationships reflects the order of causality in the natural world, where entities have a stronger influence on the things in their proximity.[49]

CONCLUSION

In *Laudato Si*, Pope Francis laments that in our world there is often a "disproportionate and unruly growth of many cities." He says, "Neighbourhoods, even those recently built, are congested, chaotic and lacking in sufficient green space. We were not meant to be inundated by cement, asphalt, glass and metal, and deprived of physical contact with nature."[50] After our discussion of Aquinas's understanding of the imitation of nature, we can see these statements as much more than pious platitudes. Aquinas presents the natural world as a primordial source of moral education. It is not simply that the natural world manifests itself as worthy of respect and hence demands stewardship. The natural world "speaks" to us about God, and, according to Aquinas, the practical order that we must institute in our moral and political lives is a reflection of an order in the natural world that we do not institute, but merely behold. We have seen that we cannot understand this concept in a simplistic way; it is not that the world of nature itself becomes the first rule of human action. For Aquinas, it is reason that is the rule of human action,[51] but human reason discovers a "model" of order in the natural world. We naturally strive to replicate this model of order in our artistic, moral, and political lives, and in this sense the rule of human reason regulating our practical life is taken from the order of created things. Thus, Aquinas says that our ability to structure our artistic, moral, and political lives depends upon our "prior" encounter with the order constitutive of the world of nature.[52]

In closing, I suggest that the doctrine of the imitation of nature pertains to Aquinas's account of the promulgation of the natural law.[53] That is, the imitation of nature helps us see how fundamental moral obligations are originally discovered by human agents, and it also helps us to see how moral and political interaction is possible for human beings. Candace Vogler calls this latter issue "the promulgation problem." She says, "The promulgation problem just is the problem of explaining our capacity for ethically sound interaction."[54] She stipulates that the problem, which she says remains unsolved, includes the demand to explain how different human agents can be seen as acting from the "same source." She also says that the promulgation problem "is to explain the common source that will make sense of ethically sound interaction among persons who have very little in common."[55] Vogler says that this problem forces us to confront a question more basic than "Why be moral?" She says that the promulgation problem presents us with the following question: "What makes ethical conduct essentially possible and problematic for us?"[56]

Aquinas's doctrine of the imitation of nature, while in need of further development, can be seen as part of an answer to Vogler's "promulgation problem." For Thomas, ethical conduct is possible for human agents partly because God indirectly instructs us through the dynamism of the natural world.[57]

NOTES

1. *Laudato Si'*, 11.
2. Ibid., 117. See also, 33, 85, 97, and 221.
3. Allan Bloom, *Love and Friendship* (New York: Simon and Schuster, 1993), 107.
4. René Descartes, *Discourse on the Method for Conducting One's Reason Well and for Seeking the Truth in the Sciences*, trans. Donald A. Cress (Cambridge: Hackett Publishing Company, 1998), 35.
5. For Descartes's claim that substantial forms are not necessary to understand

the nature of corporal substances, see his comments in *Meteorology*, Discourse I, in *The Philosophical Writings of Descartes*, trans. John Cottingham, Robert Stoothoff, and Dugald Murdoch, with the correspondence translated in part by Anthony Kenny, 3 vols. (Cambridge: Cambridge University Press, 1991), 2:173n2. See also his letter to Henricus Regius, where Descartes says that substantial forms are not needed to explain the causes of natural things and hence can be fruitfully rejected. Ibid., 3:205. See Daniel E. Flage and Clarence A. Bonnen, "Descartes on Causation," *The Review of Metaphysics* 50 (1997): 841-872.
6. René Descartes, *Discourse on Method and Meditations on First Philosophy*, trans. Donald A. Cress (Indianapolis: Hackett Publishing Company: 1998), "Meditation IV," 55. The quotation comes from page 82 of the Cress translation.
7. Dennis Des Chene, *Physiologia: Natural Philosophy in Late Aristotelian and Cartesian Thought* (Ithaca, N.Y.: Cornell University Press, 1996), 391.
8. Robert Sokolowski, "What is Natural Law: Human Purposes and Natural Ends," *The Thomist* 68 (2004): 509.
9. Des Chene, *Physiologia*, 391.
10. Robert Sokolowski, "Discovery and Obligation in Natural Law," in *Natural Moral Law in Contemporary Society*, ed. Holger Zaborowski, (Washington, DC: The Catholic University of America Press, 2010), 34. In this article, Sokolowski uses the work of Des Chene to illustrate the importance of recovering the doctrine of natural ends and distinguishing natural ends from human purposes.
11. Des Chene, *Physiologia*, 391.
12. Ibid., 398.
13. John Locke, *Second Treatise of Government* (Indianapolis: Hackett Publishing Company, 1980), § 26.
14. Ibid., § 27.
15. Ibid., § 40. Italics original.
16. Ibid., § 42. Italics original. See Daniel Russell, "Locke on Land and Labor," *Philosophical Studies* 117 (2004): 303-325. On p. 320, Russell says that "Locke's conception(s) of waste . . . must be revised."
17. Jedediah Purdy, *After Nature: A Politics for the Anthropocene* (Cambridge: Harvard University Press, 2015), 271. I wish to thank Jennifer Frey for bringing the issue of post-humanism as well as Purdy's work to my attention.
18. Ibid., 272.
19. Ibid., 271.
20. Ibid., 273.
21. Ibid., 274.
22. *Laudato Si'*, 92.
23. Yves Simon, *The Tradition of Natural Law: A Philosopher's Reflections*, ed. Vukan Kuic (New York, Fordham University Press, 1992), 4.

24. Ibid., 129. Thomas Smith says, "While natural law is a notoriously equivocal concept, most adherents hold that natural law is accessible to human reason across time and cultures and therefore that it can inform political practice by providing a shared horizon of meaning for people of different faiths without relying on mutually incompatible conceptions of divine revelation that might lead to internecine warfare." See Smith, "The Order of Presentation and the Order of Understanding in Aquinas's Account of Law," *The Review of Politics* 57 (1995): 608.
25. Russell Hittinger, *The First Grace: Rediscovering the Natural Law in a Post-Christian World* (Wilmington: ISI Books, 2003), xvi.
26. Russell Hittinger, "Yves R. Simon on Law, Nature, and Practical Reason," in *Acquaintance with the Absolute: The Philosophy of Yves R. Simon*, ed. Anthony O. Simon (New York: Fordham University Press, 1998), 101-102. The text from Hittinger continues, "Simon held that all three foci – law first in propositions, law first in things, and law ultimately in the mind of a divine lawgiver – provide distinct grounds for philosophical reflection. For this reason, the study of natural law cannot be a simple endeavor. Even apart from complications of history and the great variety of doctrinal contexts, the subject is inherently multifaceted. Philosophers who have focused variously, if sometimes myopically, on natural law chiefly as a problem of moral epistemology, or of nature, or of divine legislation can claim to address some legitimate piece of the subject."
27. *Physics*, Book II, 192b8-18. Unless otherwise noted, all translations of Aristotle are from *The Complete Works of Aristotle: The Revised Oxford Translation*, ed. Jonathan Barnes (Princeton: Princeton University Press, 1984). See Sean Kelsey, "Aristotle's Definition of Nature," *Oxford Studies in Ancient Philosophy* 25 (2003): 59-87.
28. Locke, *Second Treatise*, § 6 and 57.
29. See Jean Jacques Rousseau, *Discourse on the Origin of Inequality*, trans. Donald A. Cress (Indianapolis: Hackett Publishing Company, 1992), Preface, p. 13.
30. See *Summa theologiae* (St), I-II, q. 93, a. 3; I-II, q. 91, a. 2; *Summa contra gentiles* (SCG), III, c. 114.
31. For discussions of Aquinas's doctrine of the imitation of nature, see Lawrence Dewan, "St. Thomas and the Divinity of the Common Good," in *Ressourcement Thomism. Sacred Doctrine, the Sacraments, & the Moral Life*, ed. Reinhard Hütter and Matthew Levering (Washington DC: The Catholic University of America Press, 2010,) 211-233; Stephen Brock, "*Ars imitatur naturam*: un aspecto descuidado de la doctina de la ley natural en Sto. Tomás," in *El Hombre. Transcendencia y imanencia*, Vol. I, ed. Rafael A. Dominguez (Pamplona: Universidad de Navarra, 1991), 383-395; Wojciech Golubiewski O.P., "Imitation of Nature as a Source of Practical Principles in St. Thomas Aquinas's *Summa Theologiae* IIa-IIae" (PhD diss., Pontifical

University of the Holy Cross, 2016). I wish to thank Fr. Golubiewski for sharing his work with me.
32. *SCG*, III, c. 38. See also Aquinas's *Commentary on Psalm 8*. For discussion of these texts, see Lawrence Dewan, review of Kevin Flannery, S.J., *Acts Amid Precepts: The Aristotelian Logical Structure of Thomas Aquinas's Moral Theory*, Nova et Vetera 5 (2007): 431-444.
33. *St*, II-II, q. 154, a. 12.
34. *St*, I-II, q. 74, a. 7.
35. See Aquinas's *Sententia libri Ethicorum*, I, lect. 1, n. 2.
36. See Aristotle, *Physics*, II, 2, 194a21.
37. Aquinas, *Commentaria in octo libros Physicorum Aristotelis (In Physic.)*, II, lect. 4, n. 171. Although the *Physics* texts concentrates on the idea that human production imitates the order of nature, Aquinas also says that all of reason's operations imitate nature. See *St*, I, q. 60, a. 5 and II-II, q. 50, a. 4.
38. *Metaphysics*, XII, 10, 1075a15-19. Aristotle goes on to compare the connection and order among all things in the cosmos to the connection and order found in the household. This text is also the basis for the Thomistic distinction between the intrinsic common good and the extrinsic common good of the cosmos. See Charles de Koninck, *The Primacy of the Common Good Against the Personalists*, as it appears in *The Writings of Charles de Koninck*, Vol. 2, ed. and trans. Ralph McInerny (Notre Dame: University of Notre Dame Press, 2008).
39. Jacques Maritain, "Réflexions sur la nécessité et la contingence," in *Raison et raisons* (Paris: Egloff, 1947), 62.
40. We now know that this two-fold order can be glimpsed at the most basic levels of the natural world. Concerning the action (and interaction) of genes in living organisms, Richard Dawkins and others have attempted to justify atheistic, radical Darwinism on the basis of the so-called "selfish gene." Such a gene is seen to be the engine of evolution, and it operates simply by "selfishly" competing against all other elements in its environment in order to secure its survival. This is the survival of the fittest on the most fundamental biological level. Without getting into the details of the Creation-Evolution debate, it is interesting for our purposes to note that this idea of the selfish gene would basically oppose the two levels of order in nature; it would in fact eliminate the second level of order by exalting the first. However, consider the following statement from Francis Collins, the former leader of the Human Genome Project. When asked about the interpretation of evolution only in terms of the survival of the "selfish gene," he responded, "That's much too narrow a view. A gene is just a packet of DNA . . . say it's a gene that codes for a protein, that protein doesn't operate in a vacuum, it interacts with others. And so evolution actually acts on the organism, or even on a group of organisms. And so, I don't think one can understand natural selection in anything like its real force by reducing it to something as simple as the selfish gene, as

if that's the only unit that's at work there." My point is simply to underline the two-fold ordering of nature that is present even at the most fundamental levels of life, an order that modern science has helped uncover. See Francis Collins as quoted in Conor Cunningham, "Did Darwin Kill God," http://www.bbc.co.uk/programmes/b00jhfwt (accessed October 9, 2016).

41. Aquinas, *Sententia libri Politicorum (In Polit.)*, pr., 3.
42. *In Polit.*, pr., 4.
43. Aquinas says that this ontological part to whole structure is also reflected in our moral thinking and willing. He says, "The will of a man willing some particular good is not right, unless he refers that [particular good] to the common good as to an end, since even the natural appetite of any part is ordered to the common good of the whole." See *St*, I-II, q. 19, a.10.
44. Aquinas, *De regno ad regem Cypri*, Book I, 1, n. 4. See also St, I-II, q. 72, a. 4.
45. *In Polit.*, pr., n. 4.
46. Seeing nature as the artwork of God need not lead us to the conclusion that we have "de-natured nature." Aquinas says, "It is clear that nature is nothing but the ratio of a certain kind of art, namely the divine art, impressed in things, by which these things are moved to a determinate end. It is as if the shipbuilder were able to give to timbers that by which they would move themselves to take the form of a ship." *In Phys.*, liber II, lect. 14, n. 268. (Pope Francis quotes this text in *Laudato Si'*, 80.) Aquinas's example of the self-organizing ship illuminates a central tenet of the Christian philosophical understanding of creation. Rather than "de-naturing" nature, Aquinas's doctrine of creation leaves the integrity of natural necessities and excellences in place.
47. Lawrence Dewan, *Wisdom, Law, and Virtue: Essays in Thomistic Ethics* (New York: Fordham University Press, 2008), 212.
48. See *St*, II-II, 104, a. 1.
49. See *St*, II-II, q. 31, a. 3.
50. *Laudato Si'*, 44.
51. See *St*, I-II, q. 90, a. 1; I-II, q. 1, a. 1.
52. Here again, "prior" should not be taken primarily in a temporal sense, but rather an ontological and permanent one. See p. 116 above.
53. See *St*, I-II, q. 90, a. 4.
54. Candace Vogler, "Modern Moral Philosophy Again: Isolating the Promulgation Problem," *Proceedings of the Aristotelian Society* 106 (2006): 354.
55. Ibid., 363.
56. Ibid.
57. I wish to thank Russell Hittinger and Stephen Brock for philosophical conversations about natural law and the imitation of nature that enabled me to see the importance of these issues and how they are connected, and I wish to thank Jennifer Frey for insightful comments on this paper.

REVIEW OF *CONSCIENCE AND ITS ENEMIES: CONFRONTING THE DOGMAS OF LIBERAL SECULARISM* BY ROBERT P. GEORGE
(INTERCOLLEGIATE STUDIES INSTITUTE, 2016)

By Matthew Minerd

This revised edition of *Conscience and Its Enemies* offers readers a lucid and broad-ranging collection of essays from the generous and human pen of Robert George. Thematically, the text articulates George's contention that the values of social/moral conservatism *must* go hand-in-hand with the concerns of limited-government conservatives aiming to sustain a free and non-coercive body politic (and marketplace). He believes, and convincingly argues, that these two strands of conservatism have common foes precisely because they have common principles—e.g. respect for the human person, acknowledgment of the importance of personal responsibility, and awareness of the great liberties guaranteed by the recognition of subsidiarity in contrast to state centralization.

Though the text covers a wide range of topics, the essays are well-organized and interconnected. In his early essay on liberal arts education, the reader senses an important point of philosophical anthropology that will have great importance in later essays more directly concerned with political / moral controversies—namely, that the human person is not a "soulless self, governed by desires, whose liberation consists in freeing himself, or being freed, from constraints on those desires" (40). To put it another way, the dualistic "self" is at the anthropological antipodes from the ensouled human person. Human freedom, on George's account, is a freedom for excellence and for the virtuous internalization of true human values, not the mere expression of the disembodied self, instrumentally enabling the swift forward "progress" of the blind chariot of desire.

It is clear in the text that the philosophical underpinning for his account of moral thought is grounded in the natural law theories of Finnis, Grisez, and Boyle. While this particular manner of expositing the natural law may displease some readers, George does not write as a pugilistic exponent of this account. Instead, he reasons in the vocabulary of the so-called "New Natural Lawyers" so as to bring to the reader's awareness sound, non-religious reasoning regarding several highly contested issues.

In one place, George does broach his general methodology to a degree, namely when he discusses the question of religious liberty. On this topic, he appeals (albeit briefly) to the declarations of Vatican II, namely *Dignitatis humanae* and *Nostra aetate*. I find this to be a bit weak methodologically. While George's text does not aim to be a technical work, it would have benefitted from some acknowledgment and consideration of the thorny issues debated on the Church-State question from the time of the Renaissance. These Vatican II declarations stand in the context of a long debate concerning these much-vexed matters, which are far thornier than one garners from the mere letter of the aforementioned, brief declarations. Granting this minor point, it would be churlish to overemphasize this concern.

The most important contemporary topics treated in this volume are those pertaining to marriage. As expected, George defends a conjugal conception of marriage, basing his position on the inherent value of the pre-political society established in traditional marriage. It is unlikely that his arguments will convince those who have settled opinions for so-called homosexual "marriage." The anthropologies in question differ so radically that the arguments pass each other like two ships in the night. Nonetheless, George provides an excellent and gentlemanly argument for a conjugal conception of what the theologians of old (and Catholic Canon Law to this day) acknowledged as "natural marriage." I do think that his arguments could benefit from a slightly more detailed philosophical analysis of the common good constituted by the conjugal community. There are some difficult matters that he seems to address too briskly, especially as regards the ordering of the ends of marriage with regard to procreation and the union of the spouses. That being said, the text does not aim at providing a full exposition of such matters, so he should not be faulted for this minor point.

Space does not permit a full review of the other matters treated in the text. It is an admirable volume that will most easily be digested by those predisposed to George's overall political worldview. The text well exemplifies the manner that civil discourse should be undertaken concerning vexed moral matters concerning education, culture, the family, abortion, and the true meaning of conscience. Still, one who is not predisposed to agree with George's general conclusions will likely have difficulties, perhaps especially with his moving reflections on the life and work of Justice Antonin Scalia. However, for those who truly appreciated the good sense of Justice Scalia's thought, this closing chapter—like so much of George's admirable book—will be warmly received.

REVIEW OF *KNOWING THE NATURAL LAW: FROM PRECEPTS AND INCLINATIONS TO DERIVING OUGHTS* BY STEVEN J. JENSEN
(THE CATHOLIC UNIVERSITY OF AMERICA PRESS, 2015)

James M. Jacobs

One of the most compelling arguments for natural law is the fact that if morality is not based on some objective reference to nature, then the only alternative is that man determines the good for himself by means of an ultimately arbitrary principle. This is evident in considering how modern moral philosophy, in the wake of Hume's introduction of the dichotomy between is-statements and ought-statements, abjures all reference to nature as a standard and therefore has no other recourse than to contrive some other principle on which to base practical reasoning. This attempt, in both utilitarianism and deontology, has proven unsatisfactory and, as MacIntyre has demonstrated, makes it impossible to resolve moral disagreement. More confounding, though, is the fact that there arose a group of thinkers who, wanting to defend natural law, acceded to the dubious reasoning of the fact-value dichotomy and proposed a *new* natural law theory in which moral precepts are not derived from knowledge of human nature. Moreover, these thinkers claim the authority of Thomas Aquinas in support of their rendition of natural law theory. This engenders two crucial questions: Did Aquinas's theory truly embody the reasoning these scholars attribute to him? And, would this be a viable approach to practical reason in any case?

Steven Jensen's book, *Knowing the Natural Law*, answers these questions both clearly and persuasively in the negative. Jensen meticulously studies Thomistic texts to demonstrate that Thomas's moral reasoning is dependent on a speculative knowledge of human nature. As Jensen states, "I am concerned only with one point: moving from is-statements to ought-statements, in particular as this move is found in Aquinas" (7). He makes this argument against an array of new natural law thinkers, including Grisez, Finnis, Rhonheimer, and Lee, showing that they depart from Thomas in both substance and spirit. Jensen methodically proves his point by notably clear analytical assessments of alternative readings as well as through enlightening examples drawn from everyday practical reasoning. These qualities make Jensen's lucidly argued defense of traditional natural law doctrine both a work of great scholarly acumen as well as an edifying guide for anyone interested in how practical reason ought to function.

The conceptual key to Jensen's analysis is his use of Aquinas's nuanced distinction between different kinds of practical knowledge. In addition to purely speculative knowledge, which concerns things that man can never bring about, Jenson recognizes three modes of knowledge with respect to *operabilia*, about things that man can do. First, one might know in a way such that there is no inclination of ever accomplishing that act; this speculative knowledge of a practical object is labeled "materially practical." On the other hand, "virtually practical" knowledge is knowledge that is practical in orientation, knowing how to do something. Finally, if the agent were to actually act on this knowledge it becomes "fully practical." Jensen will use these distinctions to structure a systematic and clear explication of how the natural law is derived from speculative knowledge of human nature.

Jensen begins by arguing, against the new natural law, that there is a speculative source for practical judgments: our knowledge of human nature in terms of the acts and inclinations manifesting the various powers of the soul. This purely speculative knowledge is made materially practical when we recognize that the ends of those powers are not merely truths of human nature, but are goods to be attained. Jensen describes this transformation of speculative knowledge to practical knowledge as a two-step process: "First, activity and inclination are known by the effect, which happens to be the end but is not known as an end. Second, we come to know the end as an end through inclination" (75-76). But if the end is desired as a good to be pursued in action, this knowledge is now practical, whether it is acted on or not.

Jensen then refutes the new natural law's assumption that this dependence on speculative reason is a "physicalism" that sees the human good as merely biological, thereby neglecting both reason and will. First, by surveying a number of examples from Thomas, he affirms that the good of every power is the end which is recognized by speculative reason. Yet will alone aims for the good of the person as a whole, and so directs the person in voluntarily acts.

The recognition of dynamic orientation of a nature to the good then allows reason to become virtually practical. Jensen demonstrates this by means of an intricate and insightful analysis of various modes in which "ought" statements are made. In particular, ought statements reflect a necessity owed to something conditionally in light of its final cause; that is, it specifies what is necessary for as an agent to achieve its determinate end. This allows Jensen to epitomize his refutation of the is-ought dichotomy: "The question of 'deriving' an ought-statement from an is-statement has proved to be a red herring. An ought-statement is in fact a certain kind of is-statement. It describes a certain kind of necessity, a necessity that applies to an agent insofar as it has an end" (148-149). The obligatory nature of these ends is demonstrated by reference to God's eternal law which instills inclinations and is known in the precepts of the natural law.

Jensen closes the book by showing how knowledge becomes fully practical by the will. From the start, practical knowledge has been united with desire. In this last stage, virtually practical knowledge becomes the form of the will: the ought-statement informs the will to desire the end as a good to be pursued. The natural law, then, is simply that by which we unite our nature with its orientation to the good. It "is not a special setting of our nature; it is a spontaneous outgrowth of our nature.... It is part of our nature, inseparable from what we are" (228). The only real objection to the natural law, then, is whether we are humble and reasonable enough to admit the existence of a human nature that is not of our own making.

REVIEW OF *TWO YEARS EIGHT MONTHS AND TWENTY-EIGHT NIGHTS* BY SALMAN RUSHDIE
(RANDOM HOUSE, 2015)

Richard Douglas Connerney

Rushdie produces yet another vaudevillian variety show with *Two Years Eight Months and Twenty-Eight Nights* (from here *Two Years*), a multi-millennial environmental apocalypse story that fans will recognize as a mix of his usual showmanship, erudition, sound, and fury. This book includes as added attractions: philosophical pretentions, genies, gods, a brief trip through medieval Islamic theology, and a plot that promises insights on the significance of faith and reason in our harrowing age of environmental meltdown. Step right this way, ladies and gentlemen—admittance is a pittance.

Rushdie reliably produces page-turners and *Two Years* is no exception; there is always a great truth about to announce itself, a profound insight about to appear mirage-like on the next page, the threads of the story tickling the readers' fingers until they, almost involuntarily, flip through one more witticism-filled chapter. It's a neat trick, but being a page-turner has little to do with literary quality; if *Oliver Twist* is a page-turner, so is a Marvel comic book, which, truth be told, would have to appear on a list of influences for *Two Years*, along with *The Parliament of Birds* and Nikolai Gogol. If Rushdie here sometimes mimics the pedantic voice of a college lecturer or the "so it goes" fatalism of Vonnegut, he just as often sounds like the script of a Saturday morning cartoon: "Mountains had begun to crumble, snows to melt and oceans to rise, and the dark jinn were everywhere."

At the heart of *Two Years* is the relationship between reason and faith, as exemplified by philosopher Ibn Rushd (the birth name of Averroes, the well-known medieval commentator on Aristotle), and his rival, a proponent of a proto-Wahabian divine command theory named Ghazali. Which is primal in the universe, God or Reason? The former proposition dominates twelfth-century Seville, where the first chapter takes place, while the *logos* of Ibn Rushd (or Rushdie, as the case may be) limps along from age to age, too aloof to be popular, too useful to be forgotten. Thus begins an eight hundred-year-long debate over the limits of divine providence and the nature of human intellect, with these two historical figures serving as proxy pugilists in the clash of civilizations.

The only hope for the world is a marriage between faith and reason, a dream that incarnates in a jinnia (female jinn, or genie) named Dunia (from *duniya*, Hindi for world) who shows up at Ibn Rushd's door and soon installs herself in his bed. An Arabian desert spirit by nature, Dunia is more akin to a Tantric Goddess, both *Maa* and *Maaya*, Creatrix and Creation ("Because a world will flow from me and those who flow from me will spread across the world...") and she has potential as something even more important for a novel: a memorable character. "Hold my head when you're filling it with your lies," Dunia purrs when Ibn Rushd turns postcoital conversation to the subject of Hellenic rationalism, and the reader is willing to follow this phantasmagorical Phyllis wherever she might trot.

The problem with a novel that is also a philosophical argument, however, is that authors who can balance the two and create both aesthetic rapture and the disorienting *aporia* central to philosophical speculation are extremely rare—the later work of Fyodor Dostoevsky and the short stories of Jorge Luis Borges come to mind as exemplars. Rushdie's failure to achieve the company of these giants is forgivable, but the reader's disappointment is proportional to the promise exhibited in the first chapter where, until he reverts to his hallmark brand of polyglot buffoonery, the author lays the foundation for a type of epistemological Passion Play probing one of the defining intellectual fissures of our times.

Much of the remainder of the novel takes place in contemporary New York City, where the descendants of Ibn Rushd and Dunia find themselves victims of a breakdown in reality called The

Strangeness, a type of absurdist ecological eschaton: think Greenpeace meets *The Master and Margarita*. Evil-minded genies named Zabardast and Zumerrud appear intent on destroying the world, or at least scaring the bejeebers out of it. Wormholes open, people levitate, false prophets arise, a sea monster swallows the Staten Island Ferry, and freak lightning bolts conveniently fry extraneous characters.

It is not much of a plot, and the romance between the ever-young Dunia and a lonely gardener named Geronimo seems arbitrary, as does the post-mortem banter between Ibn Rushd and Ghazali. Otherworldly characters mix with paper-thin ones to create an aimless fable that goes from nowhere to nothing, and when an incarnation of Shiva Nataraja speaks in un-translated hipster-Hinglish (*Yaar*! Dude!), it is difficult to avoid the conclusion that Rushdie is hiding a weak story behind deliberate obscurity. Who knew magical realism could be so tedious?

In the end, Rushdie's dual roles as storyteller and philosopher not only fail to mesh; they clash like hunting plaid and pink houndstooth. Characters often seem like little more than embodiments of ethical and metaphysical conundrums. Even Dunia, introduced with such possibilities, becomes an amalgam of ideas with an otherworldly existence where she goes by the name Princess Skyfairy of Qaf Mountain. Schlock like this, mixed with Wikipedia-like summaries of Spinoza and Schopenhauer, engenders a narrative so uneven as to induce a type of vertigo as the reader struggles to decide if the author is channeling Japanese anime or if he would have preferred to write a philosophy textbook and his narrative is getting in the way.

Two Years stumbles on, a terrible novel that the reader cannot stop reading, until, during a prolonged junket to Fairyland, the story descends into complete madness, as a Chinese box spews Kafkaesque vignettes amidst a group of hysterical, screeching fairies. Has Rushdie lost his mind? Has he muffed the one trick that made him a marketing sensation, his ability to write books so digestible they almost read themselves? The reader despairs at all this incoherence. But wait—Incoherence! Could this incoherence be a deliberate attempt to turn Averroes' polemic *The Incoherence of Incoherence* into a trauma of reader participation, like the wheat field in *Anna Karenina*, laborious to read because harvesting wheat is laborious?

No, it turns out to be just garden-variety awful writing, but this is not apparent to the reader until she is only a few pages from the end, and then, well, she might as well finish the damn thing. Another Rushdie novel has passed, and so, incidentally, has the time. And isn't that enough? The reader wishes the author had placed more faith in his calling and less reason in his craft. After all, if thoughts are "slaves of life, and life, time's fool," then how better to escape our world's ticking doomsday clock than art, what better antidote for our anxieties than to lose ourselves in a good page-turner?

CONTRIBUTORS

Charles Camosy is Associate Professor of Theology at Fordham University. He is author of *Peter Singer and Christian Ethics* with Cambridge University Press and *For Love of Animals* with Franciscan Media. He is on the board of Democrats for Life and advises the Humane Society of the United States.

Richard Douglas Connerney is a freelance writer and teacher who lives and works in New York City. He is the author of *The Upside-Down Tree: India's Changing Culture* (Algora, 2009). His work has appeared in *Salon, Tricycle: The Buddhist Review, India New England, The Newer York, Islam: Opposing Viewpoints, Gay and Lesbian Review Worldwide, Vera Lex,* and other publications.

Michael Dauphinais is an Associate Professor of Theology at Ave Maria University. He holds the degrees of B.S.E from Duke University, M.T.S from Duke Divinity School, and Ph.D. from the University of Notre Dame. He is co-author of *Knowing the Love of Christ: An Introduction to the Theology of St. Thomas Aquinas* and has published in the areas of Thomistic theology, theological exegesis, and Catholic higher education.

Marie I. George is Professor of Philosophy at St. John's University, NY, where on occasion she teaches Environmental Ethics. An Aristotelian-Thomist, she has published a number of articles on environmentalism and also a book entitled *Stewardship of Creation: What Catholics Should Know About Church Teaching on the Environment* (2009).

James M. Jacobs is a Professor of Philosophy and Assistant Academic Dean at Notre Dame Seminary in New Orleans, LA, where he has taught since 2003. He holds a B.A. from Harvard University and a Ph.D. from Fordham University. His major area of research is Thomistic natural law theory and more generally the need for philosophical realism as a response to modern nominalism and skepticism. He has had essays published in such journals as the *American Catholic Philosophical Quarterly, International Philosophical Quarterly, Nova et Vetera,* and *Heythrop Journal*.

Matthew Minerd, Ph.L, is a Ph.D. candidate in philosophy at The Catholic University of America. He is an adjunct professor of philosophy at Mount St. Mary's University.

Scott Jude Roniger is a doctoral candidate in philosophy at The Catholic University of America. He holds graduate degrees in philosophy from the University of Chicago and the Pontifical University of the Holy Cross in Rome, and he has also published on Aristotle's *Metaphysics*.

Jacaranda Turvey Tait studied Chemistry and Law as an undergraduate at Exeter University, completing her legal studies at Chester College of Law. She followed this with doctoral studies in theology at The University of Chester, where she is currently researching ethical issues in energy and climate change.

CALL FOR PAPERS:

We are accepting proposals for *Lex Naturalis* Volume 3. All topics related to natural law are welcome, especially those that relate natural law to contemporary cultural issues.

Abstracts (300-500 words) are due March 15, 2017. All submissions should be sent as an email attachment to Walter Raubicheck, Editor, at wraubicheck@pace.edu

Contributors
Address all submissions and correspondence to The Editor, LEX NATURALIS, Pace University, Department of Philosophy & Religious Studies, 1 Pace Plaza, New York, NY 10038. Please send two copies of the paper submitted. Include adequate margins, double space everything (text, notes, works cited, quotations). Use U.S. spelling and punctuation style (e.g. periods inside quotation marks; "double quotes" for opening and closing quotations). The University of Chicago Manual of Style, 16th Edition, is to be consulted regarding matters of style. Notes are to be numbered consecutively (in Arabic numerals) and placed at the end of the article.

Subscribers
LEX NATURALIS is published annually by Pace University Press, 41 Park Row, Room 1510, New York, NY 10038. Subscription price: $40. Please send all subscription inquiries to: PaceUP@pace.edu

This second volume of *Lex Naturalis*
was published in Fall 2016
by Pace University Press

Cover and Interior Design by Rachel Diebel
The journal was typeset in Liberation Serif
and printed by Lighting Source in La Vergne, Tennessee

Pace University Press
Director: Sherman Raskin
Associate Director: Manuela Soares
Marketing Manager: Patricia Hinds
Graduate Assistants: Rachel Diebel and Taylor Lear
Student Aide: Kelsey O'Brien-Enders

www.ingramcontent.com/pod-product-compliance
Lightning Source LLC
Chambersburg PA
CBHW070837020526
44114CB00041B/1949